AFFECTIONATELY DEDICATED
TO THE MEMORY OF
MY WIFE
AND TO MY CHILDREN,
Lyman, Louise, Verna, Maymie, and Oscar Jr.,
AND TO
ALL CHRISTIAN MOTHERS EVERYWHERE WHO
ARE PRAYERFULLY ENDEAVORING TO BRING
UP THEIR CHILDREN IN THE FEAR AND
ADMONITION OF THE LORD.

INTRODUCTION

THE AUTHOR of this volume is fully aware that some earnest Christians may feel that it is presumptuous and altogether out of place for a minister of the gospel to be dealing with sex life in the plain manner in which it is handled in the following pages. He is also aware of the fact that in the past this subject has largely been left to physicians and psychologists, and those who have had but little or no knowledge of the spiritual significance of the sexual instincts in their application to the life of a Christian. The Scriptures contain the plainest statements regarding sexual sins and their dreadful consequences that have ever been put in print. Therefore, why should a minister of the gospel seek to be more nice than God, or modest than Jesus Christ and the Apostles who used the plainest possible language when dealing with the various phases of sex life.

However, while not trying to evade the unpleasant phases of sexual life, the author has sought to avoid transgressing the limits of propriety in the language used, and because of his experience and observations as to the effect of such teaching in the home, he does not hesitate to recommend that mothers place this volume in the hands of their daughters early in life. To be forewarned is to be forearmed and while this volume was written especially for women and girls, the truths and warnings it contains would save many young men and boys from social diseases and prevent a life time of suffering and a premature death.

In substance the content of this plain message has been given hundreds of times in special meetings for "men only" and "women only" and so far as the author has been able to learn, the adverse criticism has been practically nil. However, to some misguided parents who have tried to do the impossible, that is, bring up their children in innocent ignorance respecting their sexual instincts—this message will probably seem altogether too plain and pointed. But as Jeremiah Taylor once said, "It is impossible to make people understand their ignorance, for it requires knowledge to perceive it; and, therefore he that can perceive it hath it not."

Perhaps only the members of the medical fraternity can fully appreciate the courage involved in writing and publishing a book on the question of sexual irregularities, and especially since the sincerity of the author's motive is likely to be questioned by those of his own profession. However, regardless of possible criticism the author feels that in these days when many of our so-called educators are actually teaching and justifying those very practices that have destroyed mighty nations, it devolves upon the ministry to speak out plainly on the authority of God's Word if our Christian homes and institutions are to be kept from topping into the awful abyss of national perdition that awaits us just around the corner. Then, too, so long as our magazines print no page or picture without its sex appeal, and so long as the masses stagger under a titanic burden of "sexitis," there need be no fear of apprising our young people of something of which they are innocently ignorant. Therefore, let the men of God speak the truth, "And they, whether they will hear, or whether they will forbear, yet shall (they) know that there hath been a prophet among them" (Ezekiel 2:5).

While yet in the first years of his teens, it was the author's good fortune to have placed in his hands a rather lengthy treatise on the subject of sex life, entitled "Plain Facts," by the late Dr. E. B. Foote, of New York City. Although very young he was made to realize at once that ignorance respecting sexual matters was responsible for more of this world's physical, moral and spiritual degradation than any other one thing. Therefore, throughout his career as a pastor, Bible teacher and evangelist, the author has felt it to be his duty to deal in the plainest possible manner with those things which—either directly or indirectly—are damning more souls than all others combined.

While the author has read and studied many books on various phases of sex life he has not found one writer who endeavored to support his arguments with quotations from the Scriptures as has been the case in this volume. This book does not aim at a systematic, technical treatment of the physiological phases of sexual life—this the author has left largely to the specialists in those things. But he has tried to support his contentions with the Scriptures and place the subject matter before the reader so as to be understood by all—both young and the old—Christian or non-Christian. However, the author would certainly recommend that parents secure other books for their young people so that they may be well advised regarding the more technical and physiological phases of their sexual functions—their proper care and the consequences of ignorance and abuse of these most important organs of the body.

Scattered throughout the pages of this book the reader—if well informed—may discern many thoughts from others, but so far as possible credit has been given, either by naming the author or by direct quotations plainly marked. Having read much along these lines, and gathered his material from many sources back through the years, and with no thought of writing a book on this subject, it would be impossible for the author to give credit in every case. It was only recently, and after giving parts of this message over the three station hook-up of the Iowa Broadcasting company that the author finally decided to put this message in print, although there have been literally thousands of requests, back through the years, that the message be published in book form.

However, while this book is copyrighted, the author would be delighted to have others make use of any illustrations or substance matter that will help them in dealing with people respecting their sexual problems —which are many in these days. As one called of God to the gospel ministry, the author trusts that all who read this message, or hear it delivered from the platform or pulpit, will believe him to be sincere and honest when he says that the motive that has led to the preparation, delivery and publication of this message is that he might be able to say in the words of Paul, "Wherefore I testify unto you this day, that I am pure from the blood of all men. For I shrank not from declaring unto you the whole counsel of God" (Acts 20:26, 27, R. V.).

OSCAR LOWRY.

Chicago, Illinois.
January, 1938.

C O N T E N T S

"Who can find a virtuous woman? for her price is far above rubies."

—PROVERBS 31:10.

A VIRTUOUS WOMAN

CHAPTER I

A VIRTUOUS WOMAN AND THE DOUBLE STANDARD

In spite of the fact that the Bible contains sixty-six books, which were written by about forty different God-inspired authors, and the writing of which covered a space of time of almost sixteen hundred years—it is peculiar in that it does not deal at length with any particular subject more than once. For illustration: in the one hundred seventy-six verses of the one hundred nineteenth Psalm we have the only lengthy, detailed description of the Word of God. In Paul's epistle to the Galatians we have the only extended discussion of Law and Grace, and if we wish to study the only lengthy description of the bodily resurrection we must turn to the fifteenth chapter of First Corinthians. While these, and every other subject or question of vital importance are often referred to in the Scriptures, we find that they are mentioned at length but once. If we are seeking for Jehovah's only extended description of a virtuous or worthy woman, turn to the thirty-first chapter of Proverbs and read verses ten to thirty-one inclusive. Here we have God's life-size portrait of a virtuous woman, and for my theme and text of this message, I am directing attention to the opening verse: "Who can find a virtuous woman? for her price is far above rubies" (Proverbs 31:10).

In these twenty-two verses we have a divine revelation of the outstanding characteristics of a virtuous woman. However, I am fully aware that in these days of fast living, and an almost universal contempt for the plain teachings of the Bible on the subject of chastity, the picture God has here given us of a virtuous woman will seem quite old-fashioned indeed. But for us who have grown to manhood and passed through all the vicissitudes of providing for a family of our own, it at once calls to our minds the one whom we delight to call wife. Yes, sad to say, it is indeed an old-fashioned picture; but a picture that will call to the remembrance of many a noble boy and virtuous girl, the woman at home they delight to call mother. Certainly this is not a picture to be admired by the modern thoughtless, brazen, painted, cigarette-smoking, cocktail-drinking, God-hating, unnatural woman of the Hollywood type of present day society. But it is a life-size picture of just the kind of a woman that every worthwhile, noble-hearted Christian young man is hoping to lead to the marriage altar some future day. Already his day-dreaming has often visualized this picture of unexcelled loveliness in the one whom he expects to become the queen of his home and the mother of his children yet to be born.

This word "virtue" or "virtuous" has different shades of meaning as used in the Bible. Without doing any injustice to the text as given in the Hebrew, it might be translated thus: "Who can find a strong or worthy woman? for her price is far above rubies." In all ages of history the word "virtue" has stood for the highest and greatest strength of character of both men and women. When we consider the tremendous importance of the place of women in the affairs of nations and particularly in the home, the corner stone of Christian civilization, we are not surprised to find a text like this in the Bible. The power of woman for good or evil has been well expressed by another writer as follows:

"A good woman is the best thing this side of heaven; a bad woman is the worst thing this side of the pit. A woman touches the limit both ways; she rises higher, and falls lower than man. The most degraded human being on earth today is a woman; the purest character on earth today is a woman. Woman either blesses or curses everything she touches. Nothing can hurt woman like sin, and nothing can destroy sin like woman. Christ and woman can save the world; the devil and woman can damn it. The women of our country will settle the destiny of our nation both morally and religiously."

Therefore, it is not surprising that God says in His Word, "Who can find a virtuous woman? for her price is far above rubies."

It is true that woman was the first to yield to temptation in the Garden of Eden, but it is also true that independent of man she has had an honor bestowed upon her that can never be bestowed upon any other creature of all God's creation. Independent of man she had the exalted privilege of being the human instrumentality through whom Jesus Christ, God's only begotten Son, was born into this world. "Therefore the Lord himself shall give you a sign; Behold, a virgin shall conceive, and bear a son, and shall call his name Immanuel" (Isaiah 7:14). And the word "Immanuel" means: "God is with us."

While the purest and most honored character on earth is a woman, why should it also be said that the most degraded human being on earth today is a woman? To me there is but one reasonable explanation, that is, that contemptible, soul-destroying, man-made doctrine that has been set up by modern society, called "The Double Standard." I say man-made, for in the sight of God and in the teachings of His Word, there is absolutely no justification for the so-called double standard of morals. The Bible makes no distinction, and in the sight of God there are fallen men as well as fallen women. God makes no provision for delinquency in either case, but demands the same standard of chastity and virtue on the part of the man that He demands of the woman. However, we find that society, so-called, has ruled otherwise.

"Fallen Men!" How strange that phrase looks when we see it in print. How strange it sounds when we hear it uttered in words. But, "Fallen Women!"— how different. She is written about often. She is spoken of as an outcast. She, poor unfortunate one, is looked upon as the very dregs of society. She is dragged into the courtroom and fined. She is driven from place to place as she wanders about homeless and friendless. A young man may sink into the deepest depths of sin, and if he shows any tendency to repentance—and very often when he does not—society is ready to open its arms and receive him again. But, with the girl—his companion in sin—it is quite different. When she falls it is next to impossible for her to rise again—that is, in the opinion of the cruel so-called society-people of the worldly type. For centuries there has been one law for the man and another for the woman. Therefore we find everywhere the idea that men may do with impunity that which women dare not do without calumny. Young men are made to feel that they should see life and sow their so-called "wild oats," whereas young women who are to be their future wives must not step aside from the path of virtue or they forfeit all their rights to be chosen as prospective mothers of the coming generation.

It is a sad thing to say, but true nevertheless, that women have often made themselves the chief offenders through becoming the disseminators of this false doctrine of the double standard. Many women will draw their skirts aside from the girl who has made a false step, while welcoming into their circle the man who has consorted with harlots or betrayed an innocent, trusting girl. This is well illustrated in an incident about which I read recently. In a house of ill-repute in a certain city, one morning in mid-winter, there sat a young woman who had been cast out because she had been led into the leprosy of sin. She was coming out from under the influence of a drug which she habitually used to banish thoughts of the past when she was good and pure. But her thoughts wandered to her mother and her prayer uttered upon her dying bed, that she might be a Christian, and that the world should be better because she had lived in it. Remorse filled her soul as she thought how far from the fulfilment of this prayer her life had really been. As the tears of remorse and repentance trickled down her face, she cried, "It may not be too late; I'll try this once more."

But how little this poor fallen creature realized that a prodigal son might return to an honorable life, and to a warm welcome in society, but that it would be no easy thing for a prodigal daughter to return. In answer to an advertisement in a daily paper, she applied for a situation as a servant in a private family in the northern part of the city. She was engaged by the lady and was giving satisfaction as a servant while being sheltered in that warm home from the severe cold of the winter. Being separated from her old associates, and earning honest money, she began to aspire to better things.

However, Satan being on her track like a sleuth-hound, she soon found that she had undertaken no easy task. One day the lady, who had accepted the devil's doctrine of a double standard, came into her presence very much excited, and hastily asked, "Did you ever live on such and such a street and was your name so and so while there?" "Yes," faltered the girl, who had determined to live a new life in Christ Jesus. "Well," said the excited lady of the house, "there is a gentleman in my parlor who has told me all about you, and the kind of life you lived while there, and really you must leave my house immediately."

In vain did the poor girl plead not to be dismissed in that cruel manner, asking if she had not been true and had she not done right while staying in her home. She begged, as one woman rarely does another, for the privilege of redemption. She told this woman of her Christian mother, and of her own recent resolution to try to help answer the mother's last prayer. But the woman was deaf to all the poor girl said, she dismissed her, and turned the girl out into a world that was as cold as that bitter cold December night. Having sent the girl away in that cruel manner, the woman returned to her warm parlor to entertain that—can we say gentleman? God forbid! How would he have known so much about this girl had he not himself been a partner in her sin and a patron of that particular house of shame.

Now comes the question, "Why should he be welcomed into the parlor, while his former companion in sin was expelled from the kitchen?" When I think of such injustices being perpetrated in the name of so-called decent society, I praise God "Because he hath appointed a day, in the which he will judge the world in righteousness by that man whom he hath ordained"; even Jesus Christ the Son of God, who said to the woman taken in adultery, "Neither do I condemn thee: go, and sin no more" (Acts 17:31 and John 8:11).

> *"I know a woman with tragic mien,*
> *And wild, sad eyes that speak to me of hell;*
> *I know her heart bleeds more than tongue can tell,*
> *While on her cheek the burning teardrops sheen.*

> *"I know a scoundrel, debonair and sleek,*
> *A man of ready wit and winning ways,*
> *The one who always gains what he essays,*
> *Whose passions brook no curb; whose longings speak.*

> *"But, ah, the world, that world so kind to him,*
> *Condemns her to the deepest, blackest night,*
> *Whose maiden-heart, so trustful in his right,*
> *Bore all the arrows for the villain's whim.*

> *"'Twas never thus the Master taught; alone*
> *He spoke forgiveness to the bleeding heart,*
> *From his kind eyes accusers drew apart,*
> *Nor stayed to cast a single cruel stone."*

> *(Selected)*

To illustrate the injustice of this diabolical doctrine of the double standard as accepted by the world in general, I am directing your attention to an experience that led Miss Ruby Wheeler to give up her evangelistic efforts in the churches for a work among fallen girls. While resting at the home of her brother, she was approached by a slum-worker of the city, and asked to take a jail service the following Sunday afternoon for about a dozen fallen girls. Not having had experience in this field of Christian service, she hesitated to accept the invitation. But remembering her promise to Jesus, to go where He wanted her to go and do what He wanted her to do, she finally said, "Yes, I will go in his Name."

At two o'clock the following Sunday afternoon she presented herself at the jail and was admitted by the warden. At her right hand, as she entered the prison, she saw a large room where were congregated a number of men and boys. They were waiting together for a service which had been planned for them. Presently the door opened again and the warden ushered into the prison quite a crowd of Christian workers— beautiful young ladies laden with fragrant flowers, noble-looking young men carrying religious literature, gray-haired mothers bearing the Word of God. They came bringing the sunlight of God's love in their hearts to those poor sin-benighted souls. They distributed the flowers and reading matter with smiles and warm handclasps lavishly given. Those pure young women did not hesitate one moment to give their spotless hands in a friendly grasp to the vilest man present, and no doubt they were actuated by the purest of motives, and we would all say, "God bless them."

After this gracious greeting, one of the young ladies took her place at the organ and, as the notes of "What a Friend We Have in Jesus!" pealed forth, accompanied by a chorus of male voices, the warden motioned to Miss Wheeler to follow him to the place where she would find her congregation. She followed him down a dark corridor to where a door opened to a flight of stairs which led to the basement. Up from the basement arose such a sickening stench that she cried in her heart: "O God, can I endure this terrible atmosphere for even one hour?" But she followed on, and there in a narrow, bare room, on a rude bench, sat eight fallen girls, her congregation for that afternoon. "What a contrast in their surroundings with the one above for fallen men! No organ; no fragrant flowers; no good literature; no sisterly hand stretched out to her to lift her up to the Rock of Ages, cleft for her as well as her companion in sin; no gray-haired mother to stoop over her and whisper words of encouragement and love which her poor heart was yearning to hear."

Miss Wheeler said, that, as these and a thousand other thoughts of a similar character rushed through her mind, she fell on her knees before those poor girls, and poured out her heart of love and pity to Him who came to seek and to save the lost. The Holy Spirit came and touched those sinful hearts, and together they mingled their tears at Jesus' feet. Eternity alone must reveal the results.

It was this revelation of the unjust judgment of a cruel world toward fallen women that changed the whole course of Miss Ruby Wheeler's life and ministry, and led to many faithful years of service as a rescue worker for this particular class of lost humanity. May the Lord give us hearts of tenderness and love for the lost of all classes of society, and show us that in His sight there is no respect of persons. The souls of all mankind are of equal value in His sight, for Jesus came to save the fallen woman as well as the fallen man.

However, the purpose of this message is not so much an endeavor to save lost womanhood—although I pray that as formerly it may result in just that thing in many cases—but it is the earnest desire of the author to be able to present the truth of God's Word respecting sex-life in its relation to the Christian life in a way and manner so as to prevent the loss of chastity and virtue in the first place. Certainly this is one time and place of which it may truthfully be said, "An ounce of prevention is worth a million pounds of cure." For this reason, by the grace of God, I expect to deal in a perfectly plain manner with some very plain facts that are of tremendous importance to every normal man and woman, and to our young people in particular. While I feel sure many will commend the author in his attempt to safeguard the chastity of our young men and the virtue of our daughters, there will be others who will find a plenty to criticise. But to both classes I should suggest that we keep in mind that innocence and ignorance in regard to vice are no safeguard to a young man or woman in this age of fast living. No fond parent need flatter himself that his pure girl or boy will not sooner or later be subjected to improper conversation and influences, especially since it is almost impossible for them to open the pages of a magazine or a newspaper, that they are not confronted with nudeness and lewdness on almost every page.

CHAPTER II

A VIRTUOUS WOMAN AND THE DIVINE SEXUAL INSTINCT

Our sexual nature or instinct is a gift from God, and is invested with the most glorious possibilities for enriching all the experiences of life. If mothers wish to safeguard the purity of their children, and, later, the chastity and virtue of their sons and daughters who have reached the age of puberty, they must make up their minds, that laying aside all mock-modesty, their children shall know the truth regarding their sexual instincts. The sexual instinct is a natural, God-given tendency or propensity, and it is second only to the instinct of self-preservation. The sexual instinct or sexual urge is inherent in every normal human being. Therefore, it is enormously important that every mother should be prepared to give her children a proper understanding of these things from the moment they make their first inquiries respecting their advent into this world.

Children and young people should be taught from the very beginning, that when properly understood and put to proper uses, there is nothing more sacred than the sexual nature and its possibilities. The natural God-given sexual instinct in its fullest expression is carrying into effect the design of Almighty God our Creator in the propagation of the human race. Had He desired to people the earth all at once, as He seems

21

to have done respecting the mighty hosts of angels in the heavenlies, would He have made woman in the first place? In fact, in that case, there would have been no need for man or woman as such, that is, as male and female.

There would have been no need of the sexual nature or instincts had not man been created as a sub-creator of his own race and kind. Therefore, when properly understood, what could be more noble or purer than the sexual instinct? The sexual instincts are divine commands of God and are made sinful when turned into lust, that is, unlawful desire. Paul makes this plain in his letter to Titus: "To the pure all things are pure: but to them that are defiled and unbelieving nothing is pure; but both their mind and their conscience are defiled" (Titus 1: 15, R.V.).

Is it not a beautiful thought that this sexual instinct, which so many have supposed they must fight as something low and unholy, is in reality the stirring of a divine impulse which can control and govern our lives, and is that which exalts us even above the angels of heaven in power to bring into existence a soul-immortal. It is the unlawful use of the sex-instinct or impulses that become sinful in the sight of God, leading finally to the destruction of both soul and body in hell. We know that it is lust that accomplishes just that thing more often than anything else in this world, for more men and women are eternally damned by sexual sins than any other. James 1: 14, 15, "But every man is tempted, when he is drawn away of his own lust, and enticed. Then when lust hath conceived, it bringeth forth sin: and sin, when it is finished, bringeth forth death." That is, eternal death.

It is this expression of the sexual instinct in love—or passion—if you wish to call it that, which holds the family together. It is that, which leads the young man to take unto himself the extra care of a family. It is that which leads a young woman to leave her home and identify herself with a young man for life—for better or worse. Without the sexual instinct, we would have none of these endearing family relationships such as husbands and wives; fathers and mothers; brothers and sisters; uncles and aunts, and cousins. It would seem as though angels have no such relationships, but that they were created as separate and distinct individuals. God might have populated this earth in the same manner, but He did not ordain to do it in that way.

There is a criminal and degrading ignorance among many, who are otherwise well informed, regarding the importance and gravity of the sexual instinct. Since God has created each individual a sub-creator, it behooves every true man and woman to look forward to parenthood with a fixed purpose to be just to their offspring, to have nothing to regret when they look upon the face of their firstborn child.

It seems to me absolutely criminal for a mother to neglect telling her daughter during the early period of adolescence, what disturbances and changes will announce the fact that she has reached the age of puberty, that is, sexual maturity. Not even pagan mothers are so negligent respecting their daughters. Only in our so-called civilized countries are daughters permitted to reach their maturity without the least idea of the meaning of those new impulses and emotions that are stirring both soul and body. It is not surprising that the daughter becomes a mystery to herself, as well as to those round about her. Being untaught, she is unable to account for her strange moods and propensities. She feels awakening in her being, certain vague and romantic longings that she cannot explain. Proper sexual instructions in childhood would have saved many parents from heartbreaking disgrace and thousands of young girls from a suicide's grave.

It is just at this time of life that many girls are given their wrong impressions of the holiest, most beautiful and sacred passions of life. It is at this period especially, that every mother should impress upon her daughter the nobility and sacredness of her body and her womanhood. If she is told what she should know she will not be found rebellious against her lot as a woman, but she will rather glory in her womanhood and desire to keep it pure that she may properly fulfill her God-given mission in life. Many parents are most particular as to the moral and physical training of their children but imagine there is no need to pay any special attention to their sexual nature. This, however, is a serious mistake and should demand careful consideration lest their daughters' ignorance of sex-life lead to ruin and degradation.

When we consider the fact that ignorance regarding the importance and sacredness of sexual matters is all but universal among children and young people, it is not surprising that so many young girls are going astray and making shipwreck of their lives—and there is no denying the fact that literally hundreds of thousands of them are doing so. In fact it is even most surprising that more do not fall than do, when it is well known by those who have investigated the matter, that the majority of the girls in our country are permitted to approach sex-maturity in abject ignorance of some of the most important functions of life.

A superintendent of a rescue home in one of our cities made it a point to discover, if possible, the primary cause of the downfall of each girl brought to that institution in disgrace. The superintendent asked each girl personally if she had had any instructions from her mother respecting her sexual impulses. This lady declared that out of more than two hundred girls to whom she put this pointed question, not one was able to say that she had ever received any instruction whatsoever respecting her sexual instincts. The most any of them had received from their mothers was the thread-bare injunction to be "a good girl." Without proper information, such words of caution mean practically nothing to the young girls in this fast age. Therefore, when we face the facts of this appalling ignorance it is not surprising to learn that there are over fifty thousand unmarried mothers registered annually in the United States, while ten thousand or more young women lose their lives each year at the hands of the cruel abortionists with an M.D. attached to their names. In fact in many cases it should be a D.M.—damnable murderers.

The two strongest impulses of the human race are hunger and the sex-impulses. These greatest natural forces may, through ignorance, become agents of destruction, or, through proper instruction, result in life's greatest possible blessing. But in spite of all this, the average girl is permitted to grow up into womanhood, and if fortunate enough to escape the loss of her virtue, she is allowed to enter marriage in a state of ignorance that is simply barbarous. The sexual power under proper control is capable of uplifting woman to the highest levels; but when through ignorance it is given license, it will bear her down to the lowest depths of infamy and distress, and bring a catastrophe and heartbreak to others whose lives are bound up with hers. The pure healthy glow of sexuality, which is the greatest boon to the individual and to those who may come after, becomes a curse when debased into sensuality through ignorance.

After an evangelist had given an address to "women only" during a revival campaign in one of the cities of Illinois, a well-dressed young woman, with the tell-tale marks of sensuality plainly written upon her sad face, came up to him at the close of the service, and said, "There is one thing that you did not mention in your lecture, that I wish you would incorporate into it." "What is that?" asked the evangelist. She said, "I wish you would warn mothers to be more careful about allowing and encouraging familiarities between boys and girls. I have a sad history because of carelessness on the part of my parents."

Finding the man of God a sympathetic listener, she continued:

"I was the only child in my home. Our house adjoined that of a family also with an only child, a boy a little older than I. From earliest infancy we were encouraged to kiss and hug each other. Our parents sometimes laughingly spoke of us as husband and wife, and I believed we should marry some day. We grew up in that fashion; every familiarity was encouraged and little thought of it on either side. One day when my people were away, I sat in the home alone, doing some fancy work. This boy friend opened the door and came in, which was nothing unusual, as we often ran into each other's homes without the ceremony of knocking. He came and sat down by my side, and began to kiss me as usual, but that day he went farther with his caresses. He took liberties which he had never attempted before. I scarcely understood their meaning at first, and undertook to repel his advances, but he only smothered my remonstrance with kisses, and before I really realized what was happening I was stirred with a passion that made me his easy victim. I knew when he left the room that afternoon I was a ruined girl. Though I had loved the young man before, I hated him then, for he had taken my virtue, the choicest possession any young girl has. When I saw the ultimate consequences of our intimacies, I was ashamed to tell my people. One night while they were sleeping, I packed a few things together and ran away from home without telling my parents the reason for leaving or where I was going."

"Have you never seen your parents since?" asked the evangelist. "Never," she replied. "Did you not write to them?" "No, I have never written a line. My parents know nothing of my whereabouts." By asking a few other questions he found she was living a life of shame, being, as she was, but one of the many thousands of girls who have dropped out of sight in our country in recent years as completely as if the earth had opened her mouth and swallowed them up alive. This young woman, as well as thousands of others, could trace the beginning of her downward career to a kiss in childhood, just as many a libertine can also trace his conquest of women to his boyish exploits in kissing and caressing small girls in childhood days.

Then, too, parents everywhere need to be warned against the danger of permitting or encouraging any such familiarities, even among their own children. Every mother should begin the instruction of her children early, and persevere in her efforts to keep them pure, but not ignorant, for it is through ignorance that vices of childhood have their beginnings. Some terrible revelations of vice and even incest among children and young people have been brought to my attention as a result of plain preaching against sexual sins. Especially has this been true as a result of our special meetings for "men only" and "women only." How can a man be a faithful preacher of the Gospel who fails to deal in the plainest possible manner with these as well as all other forms of sin which are destroying the souls of men? In fact, the Bible deals more at length with the different phases of sexual sins than any other, and its moral code is the only one in the world which inculcates the principles of sex morality and the protection of womanly modesty.

During a campaign in a western city, a young man came to me with one of the most horrible confessions to which I have ever listened. He told me that from the time he was nine years of age and his only sister was eleven, untaught and unobserved by their parents, they lived in the greatest intimacy. The havoc wrought in the lives of these young people through ignorance was even worse than death. At eighteen years of age the sister was taken to the state insane asylum. I could see that the young man was also a moral and physical wreck, and though I tried my best to lead him to Christ, and he did finally make a profession, but because of his distress over the condition of his sister, he too lost his reason, and in less than three years had been taken to the same institution. According to the most recent report I have at hand, they are both still there.

I had already met the parents in the revival services and found them to be well known leaders in one of the churches engaged in the revival campaign. No doubt they would have been horrified to know that through false modesty and negligence they had lost their only children in a manner worse than death itself. I have met these heartbroken parents a number of times since, and so far as I have been able to learn, there was no hereditary tendency to insanity on either side of the house, and that in their infancy both children were apparently normal in every way. These parents were probably no more to blame than many others who do not realize the evil consequences of their false modesty and cowardice in failing to take up these questions of sex with their own children.

While incest and illicit commerce of the sexes is abominable, there is another even more so—if that be possible—that is, the heinous sin of self-pollution or masturbation. As an abominable sin against God and nature it has no parallel except sodomy (Genesis 19: 5; Judges 19: 22). "Solitary Vice" is a term more often used than any other in referring to this particular sin. There are almost no bounds to its indulgence, and through frequent repetition it soon fastens itself upon the young victims with a fascination that becomes almost irresistible, and it is only by the grace and power of

God that they may be delivered from this terrible form of vice.

One of our most noted physicians, a Professor of Gynecology in one of our colleges, said:

"Viewing the world over, this shameful and criminal act is the most frequent, as well as the most fatal of all vices. . . . It is encountered in all ages, from the infant in the cradle to the old man groaning upon his pallet. But it is from the age of fourteen to twenty that its ravages are most deplorable. Nothing but a sense of inexorable duty, in the hope of effecting a radical reform by awakening the alarm of parents and teachers to the enormous frequency and horrible consequences of this revolting crime, could induce me to enter upon the sickening revelation."

Very few outside the medical profession and those who have made a special study of conditions, realize to what an appalling extent this vice is responsible for the physical and mental breakdown of a very large number of boys and girls. Through the sin of self-abuse, young men and young women by the thousands are making shipwreck of all their prospects for life, that is, if they desire success that is worthwhile. No doubt, a smaller proportion of girls than boys are addicted to this vice, but the number is nevertheless enormous, and the dangers to them are greater than that of the boys, for fewer of them are suspected of being guilty of this vile habit.

The absolutely positive signs of solitary vice are very few in the beginning. However, human nature the world over is the same, and since the habit is so easily acquired and secretly practiced, every faithful mother should be alarmed to the dangers confronting her own children. As one prominent authority said, "There is no young girl who should not be considered as already addicted to or liable to become addicted to this habit." No doubt some will resent this charge, but a word to the wise should be sufficient to put every faithful mother on her guard, and I could wish that upon investigation and watchfulness she may find such is not true in the case of any of her sons or daughters.

Then, too, it will be well to remember a statement already made, and be doubly assured that in all such matters, an ounce of prevention is better than a million pounds of cure. It is hardly conceivable that loving mothers who are considered intelligent and moral, should be so blind, careless and indifferent as to permit these things to go on and not know it. However, I could cite many sad cases of lives which were ruined by the solitary vice, but not in a single case did I find that such individuals had received any positive teaching from his or her parents respecting their sexual instincts. It is indeed sad to think that if many such victims receive help they must turn to a stranger rather than their own mothers who should be in a position to give them the information they need, but such are the facts.

Only the widespread existence of this crime could justify the following quotations from one of the many letters received by the author following the special addresses for "men only" and for "women only." This case is an illustration of how a daughter can become all but a total wreck through secret-vice, yet be absolutely unsuspected by a loving mother during the seven years the girl had been practicing self-abuse. She wrote (in part) as follows:

"Dear Mr. Lowry:

"I need help so much. I am nearly frantic. I hope you will be able to help me. I heard you several mornings over the radio. I'm so glad you were frank and outspoken. I wish more people would only be frank like that. Trusting that you may be able to help me I want to be as frank as you were.

"I am a young girl nineteen years old and I am a victim of that terrible sin and I must have help from some one. Some one must tell me what to do. I have been in the clutches of this sin since I was twelve years old. You said that children are often led to do these things because of insufficient teaching. Well, I'd like to say that my mother has been wonderful when it came to telling me things about life that I should know. She always warned me faithfully against many evils of the world which are apt to befall girls. However, she has never mentioned this sin or said anything to me about it. Mother does not know that I am guilty of this thing. In fact, I am quite sure that no one suspects me at all. I did not know until about two years ago the effect which this sin has upon one, physically and mentally. These facts I picked up from a few remarks I heard from other people, and then I read about the effect it has upon mind and body in a book I picked up some time ago.

"I have tried many times before to quit this awful habit, but it seems all in vain. It is very necessary, for more reasons than one, that I be delivered from it very soon. I am trusted and respected by Christian people as well as others. But they don't know of my sin. Oh, if they only knew, what then? I've wished hundreds of times that I could die, but I cannot—I must live—so I ask you for Jesus sake to help me if possible.

"Now, Mr. Lowry, the problem I face is how to get rid of this terrible sin, because I know that it will not only ruin me physically and mentally but spiritually as well—and that must not be—for Jesus sake it must not be. What can I do? I have made many resolutions, and I have prayed. I have promised God time and time again that I would never do it again, but all to no avail—I am still guilty. Please understand me. I have to do something about this. I can't go on like this forever—it must stop! Mr. Lowry, isn't Jesus able to take this from me? Surely He has done so much for others—certainly He can do this for me. I wish you would write me as soon as possible."

This is indeed a frank letter! But to me it is only another illustration of the hundreds of thousands of girls and young women all over the land who are suffering in silence the agonies of a hell-on-earth, all because their mothers—through fear and mock-modesty have failed to tell their daughters the truth regarding the holy and noble purposes of their sexual instincts. In my reply to this girl's touching appeal, first of all, I endeavored to show her through the Word of God, that she had already surmised the only true remedy and source of deliverance, that is, the grace and power of our Lord and Saviour Jesus Christ (John 8: 34-36; I Cor. 10: 13). But in addition to that I tried to show her that there were certain things she must do for herself through the exercise of her own mind and will which, to a great degree, would determine the happiness or misery of life. According to later testimony this young woman won a complete victory and is actively engaged in Christian work.

It is a widespread and deadly error that only outward acts are harmful, and that only physical transgressions result in the loss of chastity, therefore it is quite important for one to understand the relation of the mind to the sexual system. That the mind has power to stimulate many of the glands of the body to unusual activity, is well known to all. In the presence of delicious fruit, or a table spread with delicious food, the mind stimulates the salivary glands into immediate activity. If at all hungry, just that thing happened as you read that last sentence. That was caused by the blood flowing more freely to the glands that secrete saliva while you were in imagination given a vision of delicious food, but just the moment the mind is suddenly directed to something else, the unusual flow of saliva ceases.

The sexual organs are made up of glands which carry on from the dawning of puberty all through life. Day and night, whether asleep or awake, the breasts and other sexual organs are generating an energy which, if not wasted through self-abuse or some other form of sexual excess, is being distributed throughout a woman's entire being. And just as the mind can awaken and intensify the desire for food, thus causing a rush of blood to the salivary glands, so also the mind can awaken and prolong sexual desire, causing a rush of blood to the genital glands which stimulates them into unusual activity. Novels that are tainted with immoral suggestions, looking at obscene pictures, dancing, kissing, teasing, caressing, fondling or indulging in "spooning" or "petting"—as it is called these days—will produce and intensify the sexual desire to the point where it becomes almost irresistible, leading to self-abuse or the surrender of a girl's priceless gem—her virtue.

Therefore, the victim—whether boy or girl, young man or young woman who would be freed from his vile passions—must make up his or her mind once for all, that henceforth there shall be an end of all this evil thinking which leads inevitably to self-pollution and sex-perversion. There may be a few failures at the beginning of the battle, but by the grace of the Lord Jesus Christ there is complete victory for every one that wills to have it through Him. Get away from the idea that one can hope for relief from this evil through the use of medicines. In some cases where there may be an impingment of the clitoris, a slight operation may be necessary to relieve the tension and irritation, and where there are extreme cases of nervous irritability the mother would do well to have an examination made at once. If a boy has a long tight prepuce he is almost certain to become a masturbator because of the itching and irritation caused by an accumulation of smegma under the foreskin. Had we had a dozen boys born in our home I would have had everyone of them circumcised; not as a religious ceremony, but as a means of cleanliness and prevention of self-abuse. I am glad to know that in recent years doctors are circumcising boy-babies quite generally, and in some cases circumcision has been necessary in saving girls and young women from becoming nervous wrecks.

However, in most cases it is not medical attention that is needed so much as a determined abstinence from all sexual indulgence, conjoined to a faithful observance of the laws of health, not forgetting that source of Divine power obtainable through faith and prayer. There are so many things involved in a complete recovery from the effects of self-abuse, that it is rather difficult to say how long it will be before a young person may hope to feel the thrill of perfect manhood and womanhood which is the rightful heritage of every well sexed individual. The age at which the habit was commenced; the age when it was given up; the frequency, and the number of years it was practiced all enter into a correct answer in each individual case.

It may take six to ten months for nature to check the nervous and physical waste. This is especially true in the case of the young man whose physical loss is greater than that of the young woman. In other words it is unreasonable for any young person to expect to fully recover in a few weeks from the effects of a wastage that has been going on for years. But let it be remembered that there is complete victory for every one that will have it through Jesus Christ, and no young person is safe in this world today who is not an out and out Christian. "There hath no temptation taken you but such as is common to man: but God is faithful, who will not suffer you to be tempted above that ye are able; but will with the temptation also make a way of escape, that ye may be able to bear it" (I Corinthians 10:13).

CHAPTER III.

TELLING THE STORY OF LIFE TO CHILDREN

IT IS most unfortunate indeed, but true nevertheless, that most young people are permitted to reach the age of puberty, that is, sexual maturity, in ignorance of any proper understanding or knowledge of the origin or beginning of life. For this the parents are very largely at fault, and in most cases, they seem to have very little concern respecting the dreadful consequences of this ignorance upon the future well-being of their children. It seems never to have occurred to the parents that from the creation of Adam and Eve down to the beginning of their own lives there has never been a single break in the thread of life. If there had been one such break it would have been most unfortunate for them for they would never have been brought into existence. What, therefore, could be more important than giving children and young people a proper understanding in these matters and making clear to them that even now they are determining the fate of those who, in the providence of God, may come after them.

Parents may be sure that when the angel of life has visited their home and left in the cradle an immortal spirit; questions are going to be asked by the boys and girls in the home, and also by those children in the neighbor's home. They are going to come with the inevitable question, "Where did the little babe come from?" If possible just imagine if you can the many lies parents will be compelled to account for at the judgment-bar of God! Instead of telling the children the beautiful story of life and thus gaining their children's confidence forever, parents turn them away with an absolute lie. The children are told that the doctor brought the babe, or the stork brought it, or that they found the baby in the woods or in the garden. To say the least, it would seem that such parents have but little respect for the intelligence of their children if they expect them to believe such absurd stories.

At the close of one of our services for "women only," an elderly lady came to the author with an amusing story that well illustrates the effects of such nonsensical replies when given to children on the occasion of the arrival of a new born babe. This lady told me that while she was yet a tiny tot, a little babe suddenly made its appearance in her home and she came to her mother with the inevitable question, "Where did the baby come from?" She was told that the baby was found in a cabbage-head in the garden. As a consequence of this deliberate lie, she said that she and a neighbor's child went into the garden and cut open every cabbage-head there, looking for more babies. No doubt she was punished for her destructiveness, but the destruction of a few heads of cabbage were of infinitesimal value when compared to the destruction of the moral and spiritual life that has often resulted from this and similar lies told by parents to their innocent children. Let us not forget that Jesus meant just what He said as recorded in Matthew 12: 36:

"But I say unto you, That every idle word that men shall speak, they shall give account thereof in the day of judgment."

"But," says someone, "I do not consider sexual

subjects proper subjects of conversation with boys and girls." Of course they are not proper subjects of conversation at all times, and certainly never in a spirit of levity. But we may be sure that our children are going to learn about these things, and it is certainly a thousand times better that they should receive their first knowledge from their parents, whom they love and trust, rather than to be left to find out from some older boy or girl whose mind has already been defiled by a wrong conception of sexual matters.

The knowledge that the average boy has concerning the sacred relations of the sexes is clothed in language as vulgar and obscene as ever flowed from lip to lip in the streets of Sodom and Gomorrah. Every boy and girl who has gone to a public school has seen what has been chalked, scribbled or carved on the walls or trees around the school grounds, and most parents would be shocked to find out how much their children already know about these things, but of course in a wrong way.

What reason is there that the sexual impulses should be treated with such maudlin secrecy? Why should the sexual functions be treated as something low and beastly? The sex-instinct is sacred, for it is ordained of God for the propagation of the human race, and he who does not so consider it is a beast. If there is anything evil about the subject, the evil is in your mind and not in the mind of the child who asks these questions as naturally as he would ask, "Where does the rain come from?"

"But," says another, "I consider knowledge of these things dangerous." No, my friend, it is not knowledge that is dangerous; it is ignorance that is dangerous. God says, "My people are destroyed for lack of knowledge"

(Hosea 4: 6). It is not knowledge of the right kind that is destroying the young life of our nation, but ignorance. Unfortunately parents seldom realize the evil consequences of their cowardice in failing to take up these questions with their children. The safe way of influencing children for good, is affectionately to win their confidence. How proud they are to be dealt with in this manner. It is possible to speak to children on sexual questions without exciting them in the least. They accept this knowledge in the same matter-of-fact way in which they receive their knowledge of any other subject.

Ignorance and innocence are not identical, and if it were possible for children to grow up into manhood and womanhood in innocent ignorance of their sex-nature, it would not be best. Sooner or later they are going to meet with these pitfalls of sin, and if they are to be safeguarded they must be fore-armed by being forewarned. Knowledge of the right kind, supplemented by the grace of God, is the child's only safeguard and protection against the subtle temptations that will assail every one sooner or later through sex-passion. Proper knowledge of their sex-nature does away with that unnatural prying, morbid curiosity. The child comes to the parent asking about these things just as naturally and innocently as he would come asking: "Where does the rain come from?" If the child is dealt with honestly, he accepts this knowledge naturally and confidentially just as he would knowledge pertaining to any other facts of nature. As one little girl said, "What mother says is so, whether it is so or not."

If the mother refuses to tell her children the truth

concerning their sex-nature, two things are inevitable: first, there is created in the minds of the children a morbid, prying spirit of curiosity that sends them to older boys and girls for their information; then in the second place, they come to look upon their admission into this world as an act of sin on the part of the parents, and something of which they are ashamed. Mothers, are you ashamed of the fact that you are a mother? Well, I am not ashamed of the fact that I am a father. If there is one thing in particular for which I am thankful to God as a Christian man, it is the fact that I am a father of boys and girls. We stand next to Almighty God Himself in power to bring into existence an immortal spirit. When a little babe nestles there upon your bosom, mother, you have achieved the most marvelous miracle in this universe. Therefore, God forbid that you should scold your child and make him ashamed or afraid to approach you respecting this most important matter. If your children do not ask questions you might well doubt their intelligence. Idiots and fools do not ask questions. The very fact that your children come to you with these questions shows that they are intelligent beings and deserving of an honest answer.

Some parents seem to think that children should be left to find these things out for themselves. Well, if we were like dumb brutes, and received most of our knowledge through instinct as they do, there might be some force in that argument; but since we receive most of our knowledge through instruction from some source outside of ourselves, this contention is without a scintilla of fact upon which to stand. From their birth animals are controlled by instinct. A little puppy or kitten but a few hours old will avoid fire, poison or places of danger. But not so with the offspring of the human race. A young child would eat poison as naturally as food; take broken glass into its mouth as readily as if it were bread, and crawl into the fire more readily than it would into a place of safety. In fact, at birth and in babyhood the offspring of the human race is the most helpless thing in all the universe of which we have any knowledge. Nature through instinct teaches lower animals to avoid fire, to distinguish between food and poison and to keep the laws of sex. But nature no more teaches a child not to violate the laws of sex-life than nature teaches the babe not to crawl into the fire or not to eat poison.

Mothers may ask at this point, "How soon should this knowledge be imparted?" I should say that as soon as the boy or girl begins to ask questions concerning these things, you should be ready to give them an intelligent answer. In fact there should be such close fellowship with the children that you could begin to prepare their minds for this knowledge even before they begin to ask their questions. Tell them as much of the truth as their childish minds are able to comprehend with the promise that you will give them further instruction as they grow older. Above all things keep the child's confidence. If you deceive them, sooner or later they will find it out, and then you have lost their confidence and they will never respect you as they should. There is not nearly so great a danger of beginning instruction too early as there is in delaying it too long. Do not wait until the child's mind is poisoned by some older boy or girl. No doubt many of you mothers would be shocked and amazed to find out what your children know already, but in a wrong way, of course. It is a rare thing indeed for a boy or girl to reach the age of eight or ten years that he or she does not know what vice means.

Others will ask, "How can this knowledge concerning the origin of life be given to a child?" I fully realize that for many this is a difficult problem. It is difficult for the reason that the average young couple had no such instructions given to them in their childhood days. Most likely when they came to their parents with their childish questions they were either ridiculed, scolded, shamed or threatened with chastisement, and thus they were given their first wrong impressions of the origin of life. Horace Mann said of himself: "I was taught all about the motions of the planets as carefully as if they would have been in danger of getting off the track if I had not known how to control their orbits, but about my own organization I was left in profound ignorance." Such ignorance would be supremely ridiculous were it not so pathetic in view of its far reaching and most disastrous consequences.

In seeking to carry out your sacred duty of imparting to your children pure, reverent, scientific knowledge of God's laws of sex-life, let me first warn you against seeking to silence awkward questions by evasive answers. Do not be deceived, for by such a course you destroy the child's confidence, which leads to three unspeakable evils. First, you lead the child to suppose that some unholy mystery must be connected with that of which you are ashamed to speak; secondly, the child having lost confidence in the mother, will most certainly go to older boys and girls whose minds have already been defiled by a wrong conception of these sacred relationships. In the third place, children come to think of their origin as sinful, and all their thoughts of sex for years to come will be degrading.

Then I would warn parents against delay, thinking that their children are too young to understand. Do not wait until the child's mind is poisoned and defiled, and then begin to pour in disinfectants, as is usually the case. The age at which this knowledge should be imparted differs with different children as some develop so much earlier than others. It is safe in beginning as soon as the child begins to make inquiry concerning its origin. Having had five children born into our home, four of whom have grown up into manhood and womanhood, I can assure you that we were often confronted with some awkward situations and embarrassing questions. But we were determined that when the proper time came we would fully instruct our children in the mysteries of life—withholding nothing from them.

One day when there was a lull in the conversation as we sat around the dinner table, our youngest child, now a minister of the Gospel, then about four years of age, turned to his mother and said, "Mamma, who took care of us when everybody in the world were babies?" Naturally his question caused a smile to pass over the faces of the older children, but I can assure you that he was not ridiculed or made to feel that he had done any wrong whatsoever. It was evident to all that at that very early age his mind was alert and he was already beginning to think for himself.

In answering the child's first questions as to his origin, it may be sufficient to reply truthfully and simply, "God, our heavenly Father, sent you to us, dear." But soon there will follow other questions as to where we came from and as to how God sent us into this world, all of which will demand a more detailed reply as to these sacred relationships of life. The mother is best qualified to answer the child's first question. The father should love, and I believe in most cases he does love his child as devotedly as the mother, but in the very nature of things he can never be so closely related to his children as is the mother. Therefore, in every case, whether boy or girl, the mother is the proper person to give the child its first information concerning the origin of life. However, the father should be prepared to assume the responsibility of giving his son further instructions later, and faithfully warn his boy against sexual sins and their horrible consequences. I beseech you, for the sake of those little ones so dear to your heart, and to the heart of the Saviour who died for them, do not leave them to find these things out by chance.

The children's surprise and curiosity at the sudden arrival of a new born babe in the home are both natural and right, and parents should prepare themselves to meet properly and answer those inevitable questions that are certain to be asked by every intelligent child in the home on all such occasions. If the mother is not prepared to answer properly her child's questions, she should seek help from books and pamphlets which can be secured at small cost. The author, in anticipation of these more or less embarrassing questions, determined that the mother of his children should be supplied with proper books and helps regardless of the cost or sacrifice in time or money in securing those things which are so essential in the proper upbringing of our children. Strange to say, parents do not spare themselves time or money when it comes to equipping their homes or places of business with the very best procurable in material things, but when it comes to the moral and spiritual things of life, many seem to begrudge every penny spent for books, Bibles and helps of various kinds that would strengthen and help to safeguard the virtue and purity of their children.

However, in this connection, probably I could not do better than to relate the experience of a godly mother, the wife of a Methodist pastor living in the State of Iowa. This mother had determined that her children should receive their first knowledge of sex-life from their own parents. Mrs. Adda Flatbush, a Christian worker, had been stopping in the pastor's home while holding some special services in the community. She had been especially impressed with the two boys in the home—ages ten and twelve. While, like all other normal boys, they were full of life and exuberance; however, this lady had been impressed that in many things they were quite different from other boys she had known. When they addressed their mother it was always in the tenderest tones of respect, and when they approached the cradle containing their three-months old baby sister, their devotion was indeed remarkable. When at last an opportunity presented itself, and the Christian worker found herself alone with the pastor's wife, she asked the happy mother how this rather unusual state of affairs in the home had been brought about.

"Why," she frankly admitted, "I have always told my boys the truth, for I had made up my mind that I would treat them as human beings, and, to the best of my ability, render them all the aid I could by giving them their first knowledge of the origin of life. One evening when alone, and soon after I knew this babe was coming some day to live with us, I called them to my knee in the gathering twilight, as their father had gone forth to preach the gospel to hungry men and women. With a silent prayer for assistance, for chaste, pure language in which to teach this sacred truth, I began my story. In a low tone, and with a hand on each head, I said, 'My dear boys, mother will talk to you tonight upon a very serious subject, one as sacred as anything daddy ever preaches about, and this is to be a secret that must not be spoken of to any one save father and me.' Very earnest were the faces uplifted to mine, and I have wondered that parents would miss so much of the sweetness of the love tie that binds the relationship of parent and child.

"Gazing into the clear eyes looking up into mine, after some further conversation, I continued: 'In such a month, at about such a time, there is a dear little babe coming to live with us, to be our very own.' "Oh, Mother! how do you know? Where is it now?" 'Listen, boys, when God created me, He made a little room here just under mother's heart. Baby is there now. When it is developed, when its limbs are large and strong enough, God Himself will unlock the door, with much pain and suffering for mother—but then we shall have the treasure to ourselves. I shall not feel very well at any time, and we cannot afford to hire anyone, so you must be my helpers.' And never was a queen on her throne more royally waited upon. The two boys toiled until school time, then hurried homeward at the close of each day. Once Walter timidly asked, "Will it be a brother or a sister?" 'I do not know,' I said, 'that will be as much a surprise to me as to you.' Thus we waited.

"A few months later found us alone again at eventide. It was a golden opportunity to further confide in them, and I deliberately pulled open a dresser drawer, and there lay the small garments upon which so much loving work had been bestowed. Together we looked at the little garments, and each selected those he thought the prettiest, and as I folded them up and put them away, one of the boys said, "We just can hardly wait so long."

"Did they discuss these things with other boys?" inquired the visitor. "No indeed," said the mother. "I had saved them from any necessity of that. I had forearmed my boys by forewarning them. One evening Bert, the oldest boy, came home greatly excited and his eyes flashing with anger. 'What is it, my son,' I inquired. "That fellow," naming a lad almost sixteen, "made me so angry as I was leaving the school grounds I didn't know what to do. Just as I was starting for home he came and whispered into my ear, 'Bert, did you know that there is a kid coming to your house one of these days soon?' It made me so mad to hear him call our baby a kid." 'What did you say to him?' I inquired. "Nothing, I just came on home." When I heard my boy say that, I felt highly rewarded for my efforts in telling my sons the story of life correctly. Had I not done so my boy would have had his mind defiled by that older boy whose parents had failed to give him proper instructions in these sacred matters.

"At last the long looked-for event occurred," continued the mother. "The happy father hastened upstairs to the boys' room early the next morning, saying, 'Wake up boys. Wake up, you can't guess what we have!' "Yes we can—we know—it's our baby! It's our baby isn't it? Tell us quick," said the excited boys, as they tumbled out of bed and came running joyfully down stairs to my bed side, but not to meet a little stranger, as people often speak of the new arrival. No, no; they had come down to give a warm welcome and a brotherly greeting to that new member of the family for whose coming they had waited so long.

"Eagerly each of them greeted me with a happy good-morning kiss, noting that my face was unusually pale because of the intense suffering of the night before. Then hurrying to the child's bed they gently turned back the cover, and espied that little-one which they had desired to see for so long—their very own baby. "Is it our brother or sister?" 'Your sister.' "Our little Ruth," the boy said, and sealed his remark with another kiss."

Oh, what a different world this would be to live in if mothers would only treat their children as though they were intelligent human beings, and tell them the whole truth respecting their relationships to their parents. When a little babe suddenly makes its appearance in the home, by the children unexpected and to them unannounced, it is most natural that intelligent, thoughtful boys and girls would come to their parents with the inevitable question, "Where did the little one come from?" Because of past experience in my home, and through the testimony of other faithful parents, I can assure you that a true and wise answer regarding these things will bind the children's hearts to their parents as nothing else can do. The children would at once be made to feel that they could come and open their hearts to their parents regarding every perplexity of life, and instead of silencing the children by some false or evasive answer, the parents would be rewarded by a hearty response of love, confidence and affection expressed by children when they are made to understand for the first time the mystery of their origin.

This would be particularly true respecting the child's attitude toward its mother. One little girl, when her mother had finished the story of the child's origin, exclaimed, "Why mother! Did you go through all this for me? I thought I loved you before, but now I know I never did. But I do love you now, mother, and I can never, never be a naughty girl again." After being told the story of life, a little boy, throwing his arms around his mother's neck, exclaimed, "Now I know why I love you best of all in the world." When our oldest son first had the mystery of his origin explained to him by his mother he put his arms about her neck, kissing her in the most affectionate way time and again.

CHAPTER IV.

SAFEGUARDING THE DAUGHTER'S VIRTUE

WHEN God gave to our fore-parents the commission to perpetuate the human race through procreation, He also delegated to them the responsibility of thinking and deciding for the child during the period of infancy and adolescence, and thus safeguarding their children's future well-being by properly instructing them in all things pertaining to their physical, moral, and spiritual interests. This parental obligation continues until the child is old enough to assume personal responsibility, and it can never be safely delegated to some one else. To a certain extent the public school teacher may assume the responsibility of developing the mentality of your child, but as to what the future physical, moral, and spiritual well-being of the daughter shall be, is very largely determined by the mother.

There are literally hundreds of thousands of mothers in every land who have been brought to shame, all because they failed to safeguard the virtue and purity of their daughters through proper instructions concerning the things that are of vital and eternal importance to every young woman.

The mere mention of young womanhood should imply beauty, virtue, vivacity, and integrity of character. But in spite of what we should reasonably expect, it is conceded by thoughtful people everywhere that the race is unmistakably deteriorating. At the pace our young women are going these days, we shall soon cease to have any real examples of those womanly characteristics of old, except in the dreamy visions of poets and writers of romance. However, in spite of the evil fashions of the day, we do find here and there young girls who have retained their normal God-given grace and beauty.

As Rev. William C. Boone has expressed it: "God never made anything so beautiful as a beautiful girl. From her hair, which the Apostle Paul calls her crowning glory, and her eyes, which carry the sparkle of the diamond of God's sunshine itself, and her beautiful complexion, which is most beautiful when it is healthy and natural; from her teeth, like a row of pearls, to the tip of her dainty feet, as she moves with grace across the path of a young man's vision, she is altogether adorable. I do not wonder that the young man should fall head over heels in love with such a vision of loveliness."

But I would remind you that such grace and beauty as here described, is that with which God has endowed normal womanhood, and as I have already said, "It has no reference whatsoever to those brazen, painted, cigarette smoking, cocktail-drinking, unnatural young women of the Hollywood type of present day society." Every worthwhile red-blooded young man turns away from all such with utter disgust. In commenting on present-day laxity of girls regarding their make-up and manners, a college lad recently said, "Of course fellows will play around with girls of that kind, but inwardly they despise them." Far too often in these days, we see girls that by their very actions are labeled "cheap," "hug me quick."

It is useless to expect to witness the old time courtesy and respect of men for the American young women so long as they continue to bob their hair, wear men's clothes, smoke cigarettes, drink their cocktails, attend the sensual dances and picture shows, and be found upon the streets at all hours of the night unchaperoned. Any well-bred young man will instinctively lift his hat with reverence and respect, and thus honor modest, sincere, Christian womanhood; but for the modern woman he does it merely to hide the utter contempt that is constantly welling up in his heart against the "benameled" peroxided product of modern society.

Unfortunately, the social customs and standards of society tend in the direction of evil, and unless a girl is thoroughly fortified by the grace of God, and the faithful instructions of a wise mother, the cloak of her modesty is soon torn to tatters. Every Christian mother should restrain her daughters from exposure to the temptations of so-called fashionable society, and faithfully warn them against the dangerous customs of personal familiarities, usually referred to as "petting," or so-called "innocent" flirtations. Any normal man or woman likes to see young people full of vivacity and fun, and to hear their merry laughter, but it makes one shudder to see young girls playing fast and loose with the fire of physical passion. They are permitting familiarities that we know will ultimately lead to the loss of her chastity. The girl who allows the young man to kiss and caress and fondle her is just as guilty of his, and her own downfall, as he is. Why do girls permit and encourage these intimacies? With many of them it is because they are left in ignorance respecting the laws of sex and the dangers growing out of the premature excitement of the sexual impulses. Probably not one in fifty understand that the thrill of pleasure derived from spooning or petting is an expression of sexual excitement.

The young man might try to deny the fact to the girl, but he understands what it is all about. He loses all his former respect for her because she is willing to permit those unbecoming intimacies, and about nine times out of ten he will shortly cast her aside for another. He is probably laughing at her credulity, and is saying to himself that if she permits his advances, she would yield her favors to the approaches of some other young man. While no doubt the girl imagines these to be sweet little secrets between herself and the young man, most likely he is openly discussing her with his male companions as a nice soft little thing to hug and kiss. In every community there are young women who are pretty and attractive enough outwardly, and in spite of the fact that they have been shining as belles in society year after year, they have been unable to attract the attention of serious minded young men who were looking for a suitable life-companion; and why so? It is all because they were too well known as girls who had not only permitted unrebuked, but had rather encouraged, the most daring intimacies. The worthwhile young man is not interested in making his purchases at the counter plainly marked "soiled goods."

Every truthful young man would admit that he has the greatest respect for the girl whose general bearing is constantly warning him—not necessarily with words, but by her every act—"hands off." As one young man expressed it, "Any girl should know that the young man always wants that one which is hardest to get." Therefore, it makes little difference whether the physical virginity be lost or not, if that maidenly purity of heart be gone, in the sight of God it is sensuality, and her chastity, the greatest element of a girl's attractiveness has been destroyed. If the young women of America only knew how lightly they are esteemed by those who so passionately seek their favors in this manner, they would certainly resist them if the effort cost them their lives.

There is nothing more disgusting to a worth-while young man than a girl who is "boy-crazy." With her light-headed giggling, squealing, affected and designing maneuvers, she may think she is making a "hit," but in fact she is utterly despised by every decent chap in the community. However, such a girl may be highly attractive to the young fellows who think one so silly might be easy prey to their improper intentions. For every girl should be made to understand that in practically every community there are men who will joke about their conquests—conquests which have left illegitimate children, ruined reputations and broken hearts. Such young men will coax and even make promises of marriage to accomplish their evil purpose. They will often threaten the girls while in a car on a lonely road at night; they will insist that they should be "paid" for taking them to the theatre or the dance; they will stimulate the girl's baser passions by inducing her to drink, or by taking her to a "sex movie." They will ridicule the girls' scruples as being old-fashioned and even go so far as to threaten to leave her on some lonely highway—miles from home—unless she yields to their evil purposes. The amazing fact is that girls will often—consciously or unconsciously—condone such conduct by continuing to keep company with these young men until it is too late to retrieve themselves.

"Promiscuity causes young people to lose the greatest experience in life, that is, love. They may possibly marry later, but they are apt to be haunted by the torments of jealousy, for each knows the other to have been unchaste before marriage. They go through life constantly mistrusting each other, and more than likely the relationship is broken off later by divorce." Therefore, it is as true now as ever, that in sacrificing chastity a girl is gambling away her last chance of a lifelong married happiness, and the hope of fulfilling her God-given mission, that is, becoming a wife and mother.

Young men of the worldly type are well trained in the course to be pursued in accomplishing the downfall of a young woman. First there must be the affectionate caress and the words of pretended love and flattery—which the average girl accepts as another compliment to her charms. Then he puts his arm around her and she feels a thrill of sensual pleasure aroused by the physical contact with his person. Then having broken down all her powers of resistance he leads her into the more daring intimacies, which are quickly followed by the deliberate seduction and the loss of virtue. However humiliating the thought may be, every young girl should be made aware of the fact that these several stages of seduction are at the command of the young man to whom she surrenders the outpost of her chastity by permitting the first kiss.

The young men are quite frank to say that if a girl

will permit them to kiss her after a slight acquaintance, it is only a matter of a short time before they can "go the limit." Many young women who are today lost to virtue had no idea that they were beginning their downward career when they were starting out to have what they called "a good time." If young women understood these things as they should, and could they only get a vision of the wrecked lives of those who have gone on before, they would certainly flee from the modern dance, the sex-inspired movies, cocktail parties and similar places of enticement as from a den of vipers. What a pity it is that girls do not keep as far from danger as possible. The majority of them are like the silly moths that hover around a lamp and do not find out that fire will burn until their wings are singed. No girl is safe so long as she is permitted to attend the movies, the modern dance, smoke cigarettes or to take a single drink of wine. And the strangest thing of all is the fact that the average mother seems to think her precious daughter is an exception and she professes to see no harm in these things.

To start with, many young women probably do not understand what it is that makes the dance so attractive and alluring to them, but let me assure you that those young men with whom they dance know, and they will soon let the girls know. One of the most prolific sources of evil in any community is the modern dance. From the modern dance emanate those influences which destroy the moral and spiritual integrity of young men and women, and it is the greatest of all sources of supply of young girls for the brothels of our large cities. Directly and indirectly a larger number of innocent and unsuspecting young girls lose their virtue through the dance than through any other single institution in the world today.

I am fully aware that many young women affect not to have their evil propensities or sex-emotions stirred by the dance, but I do not believe this to be strictly true of any normal individual, either man or woman. At this point, and to substantiate this plain statement, I want to quote at length from a letter written to Dr. Kellogg by a woman of great ability and strength of mind, of unblemished character and national reputation, and in response to his request for her opinion of the dance. Let it be remembered that this letter was written concerning the effects of the dances of a third of a century ago, which, in most respects, were as different from the dances of this generation as day is from night.

She said: "I will venture to lay bare a young girl's heart and mind by giving my own experience in the days when I danced. In those days I cared little for Polka, and still less for the old fashioned Money Musk or Virginia Reel, and wondered what people could find to admire in those slow dances. But in the soft floating of the waltz I found a strange pleasure, rather difficult to describe. The mere anticipation fluttered my pulse, and when my partner approached to claim my promised hand for the dance, I felt my cheeks glow a little sometimes, and I could not look him in the eye with the same frank gayety as heretofore.

"I am speaking openly and frankly, and when I say that I did not understand what I felt, or what were the real and greatest pleasures I derived from this so-called dancing, I expect to be believed. But if my cheeks grew red with uncomprehended pleasure then, they grow pale with shame today when I think of it all. It was the physical emotion engendered by the contact of strong men that I was enamored of—not the dance, nor even of the men themselves.

"Girls talk to each other. I was a school girl, although mixing so much with the world. We talked together. We read romances that fed our romantic passions on seasoned food, and none but ourselves knew what subjects we discussed. Had our parents heard us they would have considered us on the high road to ruin; yet we had been taught that it was all right to dance. Our parents did it; our friends did it; and we were permitted to do it. I will say also that all the girls with whom I associated, with the exception of one, had much the same experience in dancing." (And why not this one? No doubt she had a sad lack in her nature, not being in every sense of the word a normal woman).

"Married now, with home and children around me, the experience will assuredly be the means of preventing my little daughters from indulging in such dangerous pleasure. I have not hesitated to lay bare what are a young girl's most secret thoughts in the hope that people will stop and consider, at least, before handing their lilies of purity over into the arms of anyone who may choose to blow the frosty breath of dishonor on their petals."

Then, what about the effect upon the young men with whom you girls and women dance? Have you ever taken a thought as to why they are never found dancing with their own sex? They enter into all other sports with their own sex only. In my experience, extending back over many years, and including hundreds of cases, I have never discussed the dance with any young man but what before we separated he would admit that he had never attended a single dance when he had not violated the seventh command as interpreted by our Lord in Matthew 5: 27, 28, "Ye have heard that it was said by them of old time, Thou shalt not commit adultery: but I say unto you, That whosoever looketh on a woman to lust after her hath committed adultery with her already in his heart." How could it be otherwise, since the positions assumed on the ballroom floor would not be tolerated anywhere else in decent society except in the marriage relations.

This is well illustrated in an incident as recorded in one of our religious journals some time back. During a series of meetings held in a western college by an Association Secretary, the Freshman dance immediately followed the evening service, and was held in the same room. Before the evening service, four students were discussing whether they would attend the lecture or the dance. At last three of the men decided to attend the meeting and one insisted on going to the dance. The evening address was on temptation. In the course of the lecture the speaker gave six reasons why he, personally, did not dance—among which was the social custom of welcoming to the ballroom floor the Moral Leper and the impure thinking young man. At the close of the service the three young men went to their rooms under deep conviction. They resolved that they would sit up until the fourth man came home and see if he gave evidence of any of the reasons given by the speaker. Some time after midnight the freshman came in all excited and immediately began to discuss the dance and the girls with whom he had danced. In a burst of physical passion he said, "Oh, boys, you

should have seen the 'Guinea' that I danced with tonight.
She was a 'pippin' for fair, and let me love her up in
good shape. If I had half a chance I could have gone
the limit, but I will get her tomorrow night."

It was learned later that the girl upon whom he
had centered his evil design, was supposed to be a
reputable young woman, and probably had no idea of
the thought that was committed against her that night.
However, she should have known what the effect would
be if she had been properly instructed by a faithful
mother respecting her sexual instincts. In addition to
that, every woman has that God-given instinct which
teaches her right from wrong, and she could not but
know that to indulge in such emotions as the modern
dance fosters is wrong.

As Professor T. A. Faulkner, formerly proprietor
of the Los Angeles Academy, and Ex-President of the
Dancing Master's Association of the Pacific Coast, has
said, "It is a horrible fact, but a fact none the less,
that it is absolutely necessary that a woman shall be
able and willing to reciprocate the feelings of her
partner before she can be a perfect dancer. So if
it be allowed that a woman may dance virtuously, she
cannot in that case dance well. It matters not how
perfectly she knows and takes the steps, she must yield
herself entirely to her partner's embraces, also to his
emotions. Until a girl can and will do this, she is
regarded a scrub dancer by the male experts.

"I have heard girls express utter innocence of
having any improper emotions aroused by dancing, but
I do not believe this to be strictly true of any girl; if
it is, I am sorry for that girl, for she has a sad lack
in her nature. Male and female, God created them,

and placed within them emotions intended to be shared only by man and wife; and if others indulge in these emotions and continually arouse them by assuming the positions in the modern dance, which are only fit for man and wife, they commit a sin against God and nature. If these passions are aroused, one of two things is sure to happen: sooner or later she will yield to temptation and fall; or, in ruined health, reap the sad harvest of unsatisfied passion."

In our evangelistic campaigns I have had scores of young women come to me under conviction, and on the point of accepting Christ, but hesitating to do so because they did not want to give up their dancing. To each of them I have put the question: "Didn't you know it was wrong to dance without having some one tell you so?" In all these years of my experience as an evangelist, I do not remember a single case where the immediate reply was not to the effect, "Yes, I did know that it was wrong." Why so? It was because of that God-given instinct that every virtuous woman has which teaches her right from wrong.

Perfect dancing, as all dancers will readily admit, demands perfect movement, that is, the two bodies must move as one. To this end the bodies are locked together by one arm placed about a woman's waist as they stand facing each other, with one of the woman's hands resting upon the man's shoulder, her heaving breasts are against his while her right hand is held in his left, he places his foot between hers. To begin with, this position may be effected by the bodies being kept somewhat apart, but almost irresistibly the bodies come more and more in contact, mingling the sexes in such closeness of personal approach and contact as, outside the dance, is no where tolerated in respectable society. To this must be added, the young woman is improperly attired with a sleeveless, low-necked dress exposing more or less of her secondary sexual charms, her breasts. From this description any reasonable person can easily see that the modern dance has been contrived by evil minds for but one purpose, and that to awaken and arouse the sex nature, and to give human passions leave to disport themselves unreproved by conscience or reason, almost at will.

Now let us consider for a moment what this means. It is evening, the hour is late, the room is crowded, there is the intoxication of sensual jazz music which is intended to arouse the baser passions of both men and women. The women are dressed so as to set off their sexual charms, they are exposed to hot and poisoned air, perspiring bodies in close embrace, the personal electricity passing between the clasped hands, the hot breath of the man blown upon the exposed chest and arms of the woman, and still hour after hour this giddy whirl goes on until the dancers have covered a distance of from twelve to fifteen miles in an average evening's dance. Oh, the horrors of it all! Could the devil have possibly conceived of anything more diabolical than his invention of the modern dance? Yet this thing is going on all over the country—encouraged and supported by those in high places and low places.

Any number of young men have admitted to me that after dancing with a girl several times she seemed to lose all control of her emotions and also her body, and became perfectly pliable in his embraces. In other words, she becomes sex-intoxicated, which is indeed a form of sexual insanity, and her powers of resistance are practically nil. Under such conditions hundreds of thousands of young girls are led to their downfall and into lives of shame and disgrace. We are told that according to present reports there are over three-quarters of a million of fallen women in the houses of shame in this country. After these many years of study and observation, there is no doubt in my mind that the majority of those girls are there, and will finally be buried in some Potter's field in unnamed and dishonored graves, because of the barriers being torn down between the sexes by the modern dance.

Don't let any well-sexed, red-blooded young man or woman—married or single—come to me and say that he can indulge in such pastime and evil not result. If any young man should undertake to do so after being confronted with these facts, he would probably receive a reply such as I gave a young man whom I met some time ago. He came to me at the close of a service one evening, declaring that he never had any improper emotions, wicked or lustful desires aroused while dancing. As others were standing around, I asked him to step up on the singers' platform with me where we could be alone. I sat down beside him and began asking him a few questions. I said, "How long have you been dancing?" "About five years," he replied. "And you mean to tell me that you never have any improper thoughts, emotions, wicked or lustful passions aroused while dancing?" "No," he replied, "I never do." I said, "Young man, look me square in the eye, for there is just one of two things true of you. Either you are not a whole man, or you are lying to me, sir." He flared up right away, saying, "I want you to under-

stand that I am a normal man." "Well then," I said,
"you have lied to me, haven't you?" And he said, "Yes,
I have." "Well then," I said, "there is no need for
any further discussion of the matter. Your own words
condemn the whole business as being sinful and of
the devil. Therefore the boast that one can constantly
engage in the modern dance without impure thoughts
or the excitement of the baser passion, is either untrue,
or a candid confession of sexual impotency. Why is
it that the long-married husband is so soon wearied of
dancing with his wife? It is because the basis of the
spell is the sex-emotion engendered by the illicit physical contact.

Allow me to further warn you mothers, daughters
and sisters by saying that when the men of your social
set tell you that they can go through these vile dances
and never have any evil thoughts, they are one of three
things—they are more than a man, they are less than
a man, or they are low-down, infamous liars. If the
whole thing does not center in sex-passion, then why
is it that the long-married husband is so soon wearied
of dancing with his own wife? I could name one of
our large cities where it is declared that within a recent
year five hundred high school and university girls became unmarried mothers, and one of the towns of the
Pacific Coast has divided the sexes in the high school,
insisting that the young men go to one building, and
the young women to another.

Thousands of foolish mothers insist upon their
daughters learning to dance, and then permit them to
attend the public dances where they meet men of all
kinds who are demons of lust, and then they appear
to be shocked at my plain dealings with this damnable

institution. But just remember you can't dance with the devil and walk with the Lord. You may be a member of some fashionable church and have a form of religion but you have never been born again, or you would know that the dance is the highway to the bawdy house, disease, insanity, suicide, the Potter's field and finally an eternal hell. "Whosoever is born of God doth not commit sin; for his seed remaineth in him: and he cannot sin, because he is born of God" (I John 3: 9).

We find in these days a steady trend to immodesty of dress, and the sad part of it is that most young girls are willfully ignorant of the effect this has upon the men while they are in their embraces on the ballroom floor. If women dressed for the ballroom as they dress for the street, for most men the dance would lose four-fifths of its attractions. Of course there is a lustful, diseased, unclean crowd of men who dance with you, and would destroy your virtue if they could, who love that kind of thing, and the fewer clothes you have on the better they like it. If you women want to affiliate with that morally unfit crowd, of course, that is your privilege. But I am hereby serving notice on you that the decent, respectable men of our country, whether in the church or out of it, are absolutely disgusted with the manner in which modern women are dressing. Of course, it goes without saying that all such conduct is an abomination in the sight of God. Read Deuteronomy 22: 5.

In their search for some justification for indulging in the immoral modern dance we often find even non-professing Christians basing their excuses upon the claim that the Bible itself approves of dancing. But of course those who bring up that argument expose their own ignorance. That men and women did dance in Bible times is a fact beyond question, but the dance of Bible times had no resemblance to the present promiscuous modern dances. Dancing was a religious act both among the Israelites and the heathen nations. The dance of Bible times was danced in God's great out of doors, being prompted as an expression of deep religious emotions that gripped the heart. No instances of dancing are found upon record in the Bible in which the two sexes danced together either as an act of worship or for pleasure. The only similarity between the dance of Bible times and the modern dance is in the fact that King David danced undressed and alone before God, while the women of today dance as nearly undressed as possible in the embraces of men.

There are always certain things that we naturally associate together—card-playing, theatre-going, dancing and drinking. I venture the statement that there has never been a public dance in your community where there was not more or less drinking going on. As for the men, Cicero made a statement that is practically universally true, "No man dances except when he is mad or drunk." And as for the women it can be truthfully said that no daughter of yours is safe who goes into the world with the habit of taking liquor of any kind. She is at the mercy of any scoundrel who wishes to accomplish her ruin. One bridegroom exacted a promise of his bride that she would never take a glass of wine except in his presence. When she asked his reason for that, he replied, "Because of my experience in society, I know that no woman's moral judgment can be trusted after she has taken one glass of liquor." Everything connected with the modern dances, whether in the parlor, the school or the public hall, is designed to kindle the evil passions of young men and women. And will mothers never learn that thousands upon thousands of girls that were once pure are now in houses of ill fame because they took their first downward step in some parlor dance?

A physician with an immense practice came to an evangelist who was holding a series of meetings in his city and said, "I am not much of a Christian. I am too busy making money, I suppose. But I am interested in purity and morality and desire to say I think every preacher ought to denounce the modern dance from one end of this land to the other. I know, and so does every physician who has the courage to tell the truth, that the dance is corrupting more of our young people than any other thing. I am treating six young men right now, each of whom is afflicted with a vile disease, the results of licentiousness. These fellows are in every dance in this town, private or otherwise. They are the finest dancers and it fairly makes my blood boil to think of the pure girls of our homes being in the arms of these vile vipers."

During these years of experience, I want to say to you mothers who are trying to uphold the dance, and who have dared to send your daughters to dancing schools, that I have been meeting with similar conditions wherever I have gone in our evangelistic efforts. A man who was running a temporary dancing school in one of the cities which we visited some years ago, confessed to a friend of mine that during his fifteen years experience as a dancing teacher he had ruined several hundred girls. Suppose one of them had been your daughter!

A well known nerve specialist of Chicago, Dr. E. S. Sonners, says, "I attack the modern dance as a reversion toward savagery. As a medical man, I flatly charge that modern dancing is fundamentally sinful and evil. I charge that dancing's charm is based entirely upon sex appeal. I charge that dancing is the most advanced and most insidious manœuvering preliminary to sex betrayal. It is nothing more or less than damnable, diabolical, animal, physical dissipation."

There is another thing that is intimately bound up with female delinquency that should be mentioned here in our discussion of the safety of the virtue of our daughters, and that is the theatre and movie madness that is taking a toll almost as great as that of the modern dance. Could there be a more saddening sight than that of young men and women—literally tens of millions of them—every week passing through the doors of our theatres. The filth that reaches your boys and girls through both "ear gate" and "eye gate" can be easily imagined by anyone who glances at the brazen announcements in letters a foot high of such themes as: "Big Love Scene"; "A Beautiful Blond Woman in His Life"; "Could He Resist?"; "All of Me"; "Girls for Sale"; "Nudity in the Natural"; and hundreds of others equally as vile. All these derive their images from much married immoral lives of Hollywood girls and their paramours.

Mothers, can it be possible that you are so indifferent to the future welfare of your daughters, that you are willing that they should get their first knowledge of their sex impulses from that Hollywood type of love-life which is nothing more or less than a bestial service of lust camouflaged by fine dresses and glamorous music?

As an illustration of the danger of permitting young girls to attend the movies, I want to quote here the statement of a young man of twenty-one, a college junior. Please notice how coolly he analyzes the effects of the movie upon young inexperienced girls. "A highly charged sex movie puts girls in an emotional state and weakens, let us say, resistance. I took a girl friend of mine to a racy sex picture. It had the usual lingerie scenes, complications, etc. That night when I took her home, she was, in the vernacular, quite warm. Nine times out of ten (note that), with intelligent interpretation, the girl's emotional state can be regulated and used to what may be either advantage or disadvantage."

How would you mothers like to have some young man deliberately plan the downfall of your daughter in such a cold-blooded manner? Yet that is what is happening in hundreds of thousands of cases every day. What else could be expected if young girls who are permitted to receive their first knowledge of their sexual impulses in such vile surroundings? The Motion Picture Council has a letter from a girl sixteen years old, which clearly expresses not only her own impressions, but those of others. She wrote: "Bad and pretty girls are usually more attractive to men than intelligent and studious girls. No wonder girls in the olden days before the movies were so modest and bashful. They never saw C——, B——, W——, and H——. If you did not see such samples in the movies where would we get the idea of being 'hot'? We wouldn't." Another girl wrote

as follows: "The movies have given me some ideas
about the freedom we should have. For instance, in
the picture the wildest girl always tames down and gets
the man she loves. Why not in real life?"

The Editorial Council of the Religious Press recently made and published an analysis of one hundred
thirty-three feature motion pictures released between
January and the middle of May. The anaylsis revealed
the fact that twenty-six plots or episodes were built on
illicit love; twenty-five plots or main episodes on seduction; two on rape; one on incest; twenty-five characters
were practicing, planning or attempting adultery; three
leading and many other characters were presented as
prostitutes, while thirty-five other major scenes and situations were anti-moral in character. In the one hundred
thirty-three pictures were found thirty-two murders, five
suicides, seventeen gangsters or crooks in leading roles,
and twenty-seven leading roles filled by criminals other
than gangsters. Facing these startling facts, it is not surprising that we have a crime wave that threatens to en-
gulf the whole civilized world. Certainly civilization,
let alone Christianity, cannot survive so long as over
seventy million people, and twenty-eight million of the
seventy being under twenty years of age, attend the picture shows in this country every week. It is at these
places that most of them receive their first knowledge of
their sexual impulses, which, of course, are presented in
a bestial manner.

It is estimated that over seven hundred thousand
young people in the United States are living criminal
lives, and the majority of them received their first impression of impurity and crime at the movies. Mrs.
O'Grady, a deputy police commissioner in New York,

recently said, "Seventeen years ago when I first came to this work, it was an exceptional thing to see a girl of twelve to sixteen immoral, ruined. Now it is the rule. Do you want to know the reason? It is the moving pictures. Children are thinking lust all the time, and they get it from the moving pictures.

It would seem that young people of their own initiative would stay away from amusements of an immoral or suggestive character. We sometimes wonder why they will deliberately fill their minds with that which will contaminate their thinking so long as they live. But, too often we forget that all were born with a sinful nature and that they do not naturally turn to God and righteousness as the new-born babe does to its mother's breast. "The wicked are estranged from the womb: they go astray as soon as they be born, speaking lies" (Psalm 58: 3). Therefore every parent has a responsibility for teaching and warning their children concerning these evil things that can never be shifted to someone else.

> *"Vice is a creature of such hideous mien,*
> *That, to be hated, needs but to be seen;*
> *But, seen too oft, familiar with her face,*
> *We first endure, then pity, then embrace."*

CHAPTER V.

SAFEGUARDING THE SON'S CHASTITY

"A wise son maketh a glad father: but a foolish son is the heaviness of his mother . . . The rod and reproof give wisdom: but a child left to himself bringeth his mother to shame."—PROV. 10: 1; 29: 15.

THERE are literally hundreds of thousands of parents in this and other lands who have been brought to shame because they failed to safeguard the chastity of their sons through proper instructions and parental authority in the home. The Scriptures nowhere excuse the father for any negligence in the proper upbringing of his sons, but because of the mother's more intimate contact with children in the home, she is the proper one from whom her sons should receive their first impressions regarding their sexual faculties. Then shall it be said, "Her children arise up, and call her blessed; her husband also, and he praiseth her. Many daughters have done virtuously, but thou excellest them all" (Proverbs 31: 28, 29).

It is just as cruel for parents to permit their boys to grow up into manhood without proper instructions as it would be to permit their daughters to do so. In fact it is vain to try to save their girls so long as their boys are allowed to grow up into bad men. First by the mother, and later by the father, boys should be made to understand that there is nothing purer and more noble than the sexual impulses when these forces are properly understood. However, no father can hope

73

to effectively impart these truths to his boy so long as he holds in his mind a double standard of morals. "If he believes that it is a smaller sin for his son to be immoral than for his daughter to be immoral; if he believes in the sex-necessity life for his son and absolute virginity for his daughter, he is unfit to give his son the correct instruction in the vital truths of sex-life." In fact such a man is neither fit nor should he have been considered worthy to become a husband nor the father of any woman's children.

However, sad to say, many mothers have been inclined to condone in their boys that which they would utterly condemn in the conduct of their daughters. This attitude has often resulted in sending boys and young men out into the world with the impression that it is to be expected that they will sow their "wild oats." The awakening of a boy's natural God-given sexual instincts at the age of puberty is often made a joke and a jest by his parents and older members of the family. In fact in many cases boys are led to believe that girls and women are to be looked upon as their legitimate prey. It is high time that parents, as well as their sons, should be made to understand that all such impressions are to be condemned as utterly wrong in the sight of God as well as in the eyes of all right-thinking men and women. Jesus Christ did not set up two standards of morality and chastity, one for men and another for women, and parents certainly should not. It must be made clear to the boy that it is just as great a sin for him to violate the seventh commandment, "Thou shalt not commit adultery," as it would be for his sister or his mother to do so.

Every boy and young man should be made to understand that the sins against the laws of purity are more frequently forbidden and more fearfully threatened than any others mentioned in the Bible. Fornication, uncleanness, sexual-abuses, sodomy and adultery are all condemned in most unsparing terms throughout all the Scriptures. According to the Old Testament teachings, adultery was to be punished by death: "The adulterer and the adulteress shall surely be put to death" (Leviticus 20: 10). The Bible condemns everything that tends to provoke lustful passions and all that which drives people to unlawful indulgence.

Unlawful intercourse not only corrupts the mind and moral character more than any other vice, but it means the eternal destruction of the soul. "Whoso committeth adultery with a woman lacketh understanding: he that doeth it destroyeth his own soul" (Proverbs 6: 32). "Know ye not that the unrighteous shall not inherit the kingdom of God? Be not deceived: neither fornicators, nor idolaters, nor abusers of themselves with mankind, . . . shall inherit the kingdom of God" (I Corinthians 6: 9, 10). "But fornication, and all uncleanness, or covetousness, let it not even be named among you, as becometh saints; nor filthiness, nor foolish talking, nor jesting, which are not befitting . . . For this ye know of a surety, that no fornicator, nor unclean person, nor covetous man . . . hath any inheritance in the kingdom of Christ and God" (Ephesians 5: 3-5, R. V.). "Without (the gates of the holy city) are the dogs, and the sorcerers, and the fornicators, and the murderers, and idolaters, and every one that loveth and maketh a lie" (Revelation 22:15, R.V.), "And the abomination, and murderers, and whoremongers, and sorcerers, and idolaters, and all liars, shall have their part in the lake which burneth with fire and brimstone: which is the second death" (Revelation 21: 8).

If Christian parents would faithfully confront their sons with these startling declarations from God's Word respecting the sin of concupiscence, I am sure they will stop and think twice before sacrificing their chastity upon the altar of lust and licentiousness. I have taken space here to quote these Scriptures, for I find a feeling abroad in the land today that fornication and uncleanness is a thing naturally to be expected on the part of men and therefore not to be utterly condemned. Some time ago a young man undertook to tell me that he did not believe God would condemn him for the four or five girls he had seduced already—and others he had been trying to seduce—as I learned later. However, in spite of God's sure Word of warning which was given him by the author and others, he went on in his career of lust and concubinage until he was suddenly cut down in judgment and died in his sin—ruined by lust. "He that being often reproved hardeneth his neck, shall suddenly be destroyed, and that without remedy" (Proverbs 29: 1).

Sins of licentiousness have been the chief cause of the moral degeneracy and downfall of great nations through all history. Every mother and daughter, as well as the son, should be apprized of the fact that the so-called double standard of morals has largely been responsible for the destruction of chastity and the perpetuation of prostitution. Yet, thousands of young people in our schools and colleges are being told that there is no moral issue involved in sexual irregularities and that it is their own personal affair. Some of these vile-hearted so-called educators have gone so far as to teach the devil's lie, and young people are being told that sex-denial causes ill-health, nervousness, even insanity. Needless to say that such teachers expose their own ignorance of the Bible, history and sexology, and so far as my observation goes, the majority of our Christian parents are blind as bats as to what is going on among their children in our high schools and tax supported colleges and universities.

The ignorance on the part of parents as to what is going on in the lives of boys and young men is well illustrated by an incident that was related to me by the Secretary of the Y. M. C. A. in a mid-western town of twelve thousand population. He told me that in his "Life's Problems Class" of twenty-five boys and young men—most of them from the high school, he discovered that sixteen were practicing self-abuse; fourteen had been guilty of the violation of the seventh command— either with single or married women—and six out of the twenty-five were already contaminated with veneral disease. Facing such facts, it is not surprising to learn that sixty per cent of the men infected with venereal disease contracted it between the ages of fifteen and twenty-one, and twenty-five per cent between twenty-one and twenty-five years of age. The late Dr. Prince A. Morrow, who did so much to educate young men in matters of sex, said that fully one-half of the physical ailments of young men are due to the violation of sex-laws. "In his investigations of the asylums of one nation, Dr. Piqua claims that he found that eighty-two per cent of all the inmates among the females and seventy-eight per cent among the males, involved the sexual mechanism, functioning or both, and that early **sex instruction** would have wholly precluded much of

this insanity and postponed the mental breakdown in
many other cases until later in life."

Teach your boys that the penalties inflicted because
of the violation of the laws of sex are the most severe
in their effects upon the mental and physical nature
of all sins of which men and women are guilty. In
fact our nation is being literally rotted into perdition
because of the various forms of venereal diseases, the
germs of which are carrying on their work of destruction in the bodies of literally millions of our population. Think of seven hundred fifty thousand "fallen
women" and two or three million "fallen men" spread-
ing the most contagious diseases around our fair country! The New York City Medical Society estimates that
there are in that city not less than two hundred thousand
persons infected with gonorrhœa and syphilis. It has
been estimated by some of our medical authorities that
there are in this country today over four million men
whose blood has already become tainted with the virus
of these two most dreadful diseases known to man.
Show your son how that a single lapse from virtue is
enough to taint the young man's blood with the virus
of one of these dreadful diseases which he may later—
and even after considering himself cured—communi-
cate to his innocent wife and children.

The shortest and surest route for a young woman
to the operating table of the surgeon is to marry that
young man who has lived a questionable life and who
thought there was no harm in sowing his "wild oats."
I have always said that if I lived to see my daughters
married, no young man could gain my consent to the
wedding until he first produced a medical certificate
proving that his blood is free from the taint of venereal

disease. If all parents would do likewise it would prevent—as Dr. Morrow of New York declared—at least seventy-five per cent of the operations on women because of female troubles. As I have learned from experience and observation, any young man who has lived a clean life will be delighted to grant your request for medical certificate. But should he refuse to produce such proof of his chastity, you have all the evidence you need for refusing to give your consent to the union. I am glad that some States have already passed a law prohibiting the issuance of a marriage certificate until both parties produce a medical certificate showing that they are free from the virus of venereal diseases.

There are literally hundreds of thousands of wives in this country who are suffering a living death all because their husbands started out in life with the impression that they must have their so-called "fling." These husbands, either before or after marriage, contracted a venereal disease, and supposing themselves cured, later transmitted the disease to their wives. It is a well known fact that the germs of these diseases will lie latent in the system for months and years, and then under a strain of sexual excess rapidly multiply into millions of new germs. In fact where these diseases become chronic, a perfect and permanent cure becomes more or less doubtful. One case that came to my attention was that of a young man who became inoculated with the virus of gonorrhœa. Eighteen months later, supposing himself cured, he married. Two months after marriage his wife had an accute attack of ovaritis and pelvic peritonitis, and came near losing her life. She did lose her ovaries, depriving her of the possibility of ever becoming a happy mother of children.

Formerly it was thought that as soon as the inflammation had subsided and the discharge disappeared a man might safely marry. But now it is known that many thousands of brides are annually inoculated at the first approach of the husband who had confidently believed himself cured long years before his marriage. While on the way to the tabernacle for an afternoon service in a western city where we were engaged in a union revival campaign, I was met on the street by an earnest Christian physician and surgeon who told me he was on a sad mission that afternoon. I asked him for the cause. He said, "I am going over to the hospital to unsex a woman. Her husband contracted gonorrhœa some years ago and, supposing himself cured, married a young woman from one of our best homes and she has a very serious attack of the disease. However I am hoping to save her life by removing her ovaries, but it may be necessary to remove her womb also."

Well, as for myself, I went on to that afternoon service more determined than ever, that regardless of the criticisms that might be heaped upon me for dealing with these plain facts, I would, by the grace of God, do my best to warn both men and women that they cannot sin and get away with it. Before I made a special study of these things, it was a mystery to me as well as many others, why so often a blooming bride a few weeks or months after her marriage became a pale confirmed invalid. Often you have heard it said, "Well, marriage did not agree with her." And the poor woman suffers in silence and ignorance of the cause, and in many cases accuses herself of being unable to perform her God-given mission in life, when the fault was in no wise her own. What a hell-on-earth it must be for such a husband when he sees his wife fading away and dying in ignorance of her trouble, while he never had the grit and manhood to tell his innocent companion that the fault was all his own.

No one is so familiar with the misery, the tragedies, the barren and wasted lives, the premature graves, the suicides and sufferings caused by sexual ignorance, as is the observing and sympathetic physician. Therefore, since one of the most effective ways of getting the truth across to people is by example and illustration, I am calling attention to one of the many cases that has come under the observation of William J. Robinson, M.D. He tells of a young woman who was graduating from college in her twenty-third year. She was a bright, cheerful, happy girl, and the day of graduating was one of the happiest occasions in her life. Not alone because she was graduating with honors, but because a young man five years her senior, whom she had loved and looked up to for a number of years, had proposed the night before.

The passion and romance of that proposal was still lingering with her, as the plans and hopes and dreams of future happiness kept chasing each other through her fertile brain. She had decided where they would live, where they would spend their summers and, being a normal woman possessing her rightful sexual instinct, she had been thinking about how she would bring up her children. She felt that she had been chosen by a man who would make a husband to be proud of anywhere. He had already achieved eminence in the legal profession, and his practice was more than he could take care of. He had been an all-round athlete, and just such a man, as she thought, to protect a woman from every possible care and danger and make her happy as long as she lived.

They were married in October, and expected to be away three months on their honeymoon. But the young woman not feeling well they returned in three weeks. She looked rather tired and fagged out, but that was thought to be natural with so much traveling to which she was not accustomed. It was not natural, however, that after a week's rest she did not show any improvement. On the contrary, she began to look somewhat haggard. She continued to grow worse until the beginning of January, when she was taken violently and dangerously ill. Severe abdominal pain, and a very rapid, hard pulse, threatened complete collapse. The case was diagnosed as a ruptured tubal pregnancy. A consulting surgeon was called in and it was decided that in order to save the patient's life, an immediate operation was necessary. She was quickly removed to a private hospital and operated upon. No signs of extra-uterine pregnancy were discovered, but over three pints of a blood-stained serum was removed. An examination of this serum demonstrated the presence of millions of gonococcic, the germ of gonorrhœa. Both tubes were removed, and so was the now useless womb. The doctor pronounced the operation a success, that is, the patient recovered.

A confidential talk was had with the husband. Yes, two years before he had had a mild attack of gonorrhœa. It was very mild, and didn't bother him much. He had gone to a physician, and in three or four weeks had been told that he was all right, and he had thought little of the matter since. An examination, however, demonstrated the presence of the germs. Personally he had been physically strong enough to resist the germs to the point that he had not been seriously affected up to that time. His despair at learning that he was the unwitting cause of the tragedy can better be imagined than described.

In a sense, the young woman recovered, but one would hardly have known her. She aged ten years in ten months. After that she was making no plans, she had no hopes, she was dreaming no dreams of future happiness. Never will her home be gladdened by the noise, romp and laughter of little children whom she could rightfully call her own. The wreck of this home, as well as hundreds of thousands of others, can be traced to ignorance, first on the part of the parents and later on the part of those young people who were permitted to grow to manhood and womanhood in ignorance of the consequences of the loss of chastity.

Unpleasant though this subject may be to many readers, I feel that I should not leave it without a word of warning respecting syphilis, the most serious of all venereal diseases. It is caused by germs which are carried in the blood through the whole body. There is perhaps nothing known to the medical profession so horrible and insidious as syphilis. As expressed by Thurman B. Rice, M.D., "Because it can destroy health and shorten effective life; because it can undermine homes and break up families; because it is a potent source of sterility; because it decreases the efficiency of workers and breadwinners; because it entails great expense for treatment and hospital care; and because it enormously complicates and sophisticates the environment in which men, women and children must live, venereal disease must be described as one of the greatest, if not the greatest, of the many social problems which so perplex those who have at heart the welfare of the race and nation. It is difficult to believe that any nation can long continue to be great if it is badly contaminated with these diseases."

Syphilis ranks high if not actually first among causes of death. It is most absurd to spend hundreds of millions of dollars for the conservation of the country's physical resources while neglecting the most valuable of all the natural resources, that is, the human mind and body. Dr. Cutter's recent public discussion of syphilis must have come as a shock to the laymen who have given so little thought to the subject. He reported that each year half a million new cases of the disease occur in this country. He reported that in eight years the number of cases of syphilis exceeded the number of cases of tuberculosis by nearly a million. The record is an appalling one, particularly in view of the devastating nature of the disease to those who contract it and to their offspring.

The germs of syphilis being more closely related to the animal kingdom than any other disease—producing bacteria—they may live for months and years in the infected tissues of the body. Then, uncured syphilis may destroy any part of the body tissues— the bones, muscles, teeth, nerves and the blood vessels. The germs of this horrible disease are usually brought into the system through immoral and illicit-sexual congress and prostitution, but may be transmitted when the living germs get into a broken place in the skin or mucous membrane through kissing and other intimate contacts. A Chicago physician tells how a young woman who had a slight abrasion on her lip, contracted the disease by permitting a young man to kiss her good night after taking her home from a place of amusement. Inside of three years, through ignorance and improper treatment she had rotted into her grave, another victim of this horrible disease. Dr. F. J. Farnell reports eight cases from Philadelphia that were traced to a kissing social.

Syphilis is generally described as acquired and hereditary. It may be transmitted from parent to child, and this disease takes the same course in women as in men. Sin has a method of punishing its victim, for nature will not permit her sacred laws to be violated, and her punishment is severe. The final stages may appear at any time up to twenty years or more after the early active stages. It may attack any organ of the body, and in its later stages cause Paresis (softening of the brain), and other forms of insanity. It may also produce locomotor ataxia, early apoplexy, paralysis, blindness, deafness, liver or heart disease and deformity of bones and joints.

Many a fine young man and woman have gone down in modern times because of this horrible disease. Many of royal blood have been victims of this destructive germ. Karl the 8th, Ludvig the 12th, Philip the 2nd of Spain, Ludvig the 14th and 15th, August of Saxony, Fredrick Wilhelm of Prussia and a number of the popes were victims of this disease. Friedrich Nietzsche, Germany's great philosopher, wrote his last work, "Ecce Homo," while this terrible disease was bursting forth over his entire body. Some of his horrible philosophies were written while violently insane because of syphilis, and he, as well as many others prominent in world affairs, found the Bible true when it declares, "The wages of sin is death."

The germs of syphilis once having entered the system, every organ in the body may be attacked and partly disorganized. During this time appropriate treatment may do much to help control the symptoms and it may even appear that the disease has been cured. But very often this is only an apparent cure. Unless the most efficient remedy, which is tedious, slow, expensive and frequently painful, be followed for a long period, the disease may show itself in a renewed attack later in almost any part of the body. This is because the syphilitic virus possesses the most remarkable power of remaining quiet for years and then beginning to cause trouble again. Without energetic and long drawn out treatment the patient infected with this disease may expect to become progressively worse until utterly incapaciated and fatally affected. The patient should not think of stopping treatments until repeated blood tests indicate that the disease is probably cured or at least definitely arrested.

If we are to hope for an ultimate improvement of our race physically, no person should marry who has been infected with syphilis until he can be given proof positive that no further signs of the disease exist in blood or spinal fluid. The grace of God is sufficient to save the deepest dyed sinner on earth when he surrenders himself to Jesus Christ for salvation, but that does not mean that those portions of his body which have decayed and sloughed away because of sin and disease, will be restored. A man may have lost a limb in some form of accident while under the influence of liquor, but becoming a saved man does not mean that that member of his body will be restored. He is saved from the guilt and final penalty of his sin, but he must go through life constantly confronted with the consequences of his sin and selfishness. I have met many men in my travels whom I have considered to be thoroughly and soundly converted but because of sexual sins of one kind and another, they have a lifetime of suffering ahead of them.

However, the purpose of this chapter is not to suggest remedies and methods of treatment, but rather to help parents in safeguarding the chastity of their sons. If they have already become contaminated, the best medical advice possible should be obtained at once. But before leaving this unpleasant subject, I want to add a word of warning respecting the hereditary effects of this terrible disease in the bodies of innocent wives and children. Many wives contract the disease from their husbands, and then it is contracted from the mother by the child while in the womb. Usually children born of syphilitic mothers are seriously damaged physically and their chances for normal development are greatly reduced. If the mother has a severe attack of the disease, and it is in its early stages, the child is almost certain to die before birth. The father does not give the disease to the child, but to the mother, who gives it to the child, causing it to be born with the infection. I might call attention to incidents that have come under my personal observation back through the years, but I believe one from the records of an experienced physician will be more acceptable as proving this point.

The following sad case was reported by Dr. Oswald C. J. Withrow. A brilliant and accomplished girl married a soldier just before he sailed for service abroad during the great World War. She knew that he had lived a rather fast life. Her mother knew it too. But the girl's love for him was so great that everything else was lost sight of because of her ignorance of the consequences of marrying a young man who believed in the double standard.

The father was across the sea when the baby was born. As the months went by the young wife noticed something strange about her child, and when he was two years old she brought him to Dr. Withrow for examination and advice. The baby was found to be a helpless, hopeless idiot, and the young mother was suffering from that hideous, loathsome and devastating disease, syphilis. The mother, after having undergone a long and expensive treatment, has reason to hope she has been cured. The baby, however, will be a helpless, hopeless idiot until death shall mercifully remove it from being an incubus to the mother and to society. In the meantime the crime of the father curses his nation, from which he went to fight in the struggle for liberty and freedom.

God forbid that it should be so, but it is quite possible that your sons may be called to enlist in future warfare. Are you parents willing that they should go out from your home in their ignorance concerning the consequences of sexual sins as did hundreds of thousands of the young men who fought in the last great war? During the transportation of the Canadian troops, a delay of some days occurred at Halifax, waiting for the steamer that was to take them abroad. It was said that men, wine and women mixed quite freely in the dances and other methods of amusement, with the result that out of five hundred of Canada's brightest and best sons, one hundred fifty were ill with venereal disease on the voyage, one became insane, one died, while ten others were so serious they were refused the privilege of going to the front when they landed.

This is another illustration of the worst of all consequences of the modern dance—if there can be one particular thing worse than those mentioned in the former chapter—the fact that it has become one of the most prolific sources for the spread of venereal diseases. Even if your daughter is not ruined by the dance, if she attends them at all, most likely she will marry a man who has been a devotee of the dance hall where he may contract one of these diseases. In one of the cities where we held a revival campaign some time ago, I learned of a girl who was ruined in the modern dance, where she contracted gonorrhœa. She became morose and revengeful, refusing medical treatment. I was told that in less than six months she had wilfully transmitted this disease to fifteen young men in that community. Many husbands have contracted these diseases at the dance hall and later transmitted it to their innocent wives.

Facing these horrible consequences of the double standard, every parent, every teacher, every minister and spiritual advisor, should not fail to see to it that growing youths are properly instructed and warned before they meet with and accept those temptations which are certain to assail them. There is no longer any reason why public opinion should be permitted to stamp these shameful diseases as unmentionable, and thus drive the victims into hiding, where they can secretly carry on their work of destruction unsuspected by the youth of a so-called Christian nation. Therefore let every Christian father and mother rally to the support of those faithful men and women of the medical profession who have recently been doing all in their power to awaken public sentiment in favor of making these facts known, for our Lord has said, "My people are destroyed for lack of knowledge" (Hosea 4: 6).

The Chicago Tribune is certainly to be commended for the publicity it has been giving to the prevalence of venereal diseases, and its editors are largely responsible for certain laws that have been passed in Illinois that I trust will shortly become general throughout the United States. The following quotation is from an editorial that appeared in that great daily, February 2, 1938:

"Why must we fight this fight? Because syphilis and gonorrhœa, in the words of the title of a notable book by Dr. Parran, is a 'shadow on the land,' and one of the widest and blackest. His summary is staggering. At least one-half million persons, he estimates, are diagnosed annually as syphilitic. One million potential mothers in the United States now have or have had syphilis. Less than one-half of cases seek treatment or are recognized within the first year of the disease. Only one out of five receives the minimum treatment. Each year 60,000 children are born with congenital syphilis. Five out of six untreated mothers will bear a dead or diseased child. One-third of the children with congenital syphilis will develop partial or complete blindness if not treated.

"Syphilis can be ended in the United States as one of the great plagues. The Scandinavian countries have already progressed a long way to that goal. Our task is greater and it is barely begun. But it can be done. The first essential is public knowledge."

CHAPTER VI.

PROCREATION AND THE DIVINE PURPOSE OF WEDLOCK

MAN is different from all other animate creatures upon this earth, in that God created him intelligent and free, giving to him faith, conscience and morals. Other animals have certain instincts found in the human race, but man was designed for an immortal existence. Man has a spiritual nature for he was made in the image of God, and is a trinity. Man has spirit, soul, and body (I Thess. 5:23). God also created them male and female, because, from the very beginning, they were destined to perpetuate themselves upon the earth by means of procreation. The theory of evolution has not one scintilla of evidence upon which to stand. What is the sense of discussing "a missing link," since they are "all" missing? Man can never improve upon those majestic statements concerning his origin, found in the first and second chapters of the first book of the Bible: "So God created man in his own image, in the image of God created he him; male and female created he them" (Genesis 1: 27).

Wedlock and procreation being ordained of God, we would naturally expect that the Bible would have a great deal to say about marriage—its privileges and responsibilities. In fact, there is no phase of it overlooked in the Scriptures of the Old and New Testaments. It is first mentioned in Genesis 2: 18 and 24:

"And the Lord God said, It is not good that man should be alone; I will make him an help meet for him . . . Therefore shall a man leave his father and his mother, and shall cleave unto his wife: and they shall be one flesh." When answering the Pharisees concerning the question of divorce, Jesus Christ set his stamp of approval and authority upon the sanctity of marriage: "And he answered and said unto them, Have ye not read, that he which made them at the beginning made them male and female, and said, For this cause shall a man leave his father and mother, and shall cleave to his wife: and they twain shall be one flesh? Wherefore they are no more twain, but one flesh. What therefore God hath joined together, let not man put asunder" (Matthew 19: 4-6).

God made both man and woman, and He made them different. He created them male and female that they might be invested with the power to bring into existence through generation, immortal spirits like unto themselves. However, the fact that God made the woman different does not mean that she is inferior to man. God has given us "Equality in difference," so that we may travel our heavenly journey side by side, dividing and sharing alike the cares, the joys and sorrows of life. As someone has aptly said: "Woman was made from man's side; not from his head, to rule over him, nor his feet to be his slave, but from his side, nearest his heart, to be his companion, his helper, and his inspiration."

To encourage the fusion of these two hearts into a new being through the travail and toil entailed in procreation, God has ordained and placed within the human heart the sexual urge, that is, the supreme desire to love and to be loved. Without this the human race would have perished from off the face of the earth many centuries ago. Therefore, this relationship of the two sexes being divinely ordained of God, every mother should count it her responsibility to fully instruct her daughters and give them to understand that the natural outcome of marriage will be parenthood.

Not one word of condemnation do we have from Scripture against any one who has been denied by nature the privilege of parenthood, but woe be it unto those husbands and wives who are in rebellion against God's primal commands respecting this responsibility. The principles of righteousness as set forth in these primal commands have never been revoked or changed, and that in spite of the fact that the first one was given before the fall of man. The first one was given to Adam and Eve, and the second to Noah and his sons. "And God blessed them, and God said unto them, be fruitful, and multiply, and replenish the earth, and subdue it: and have dominion over the fish of the sea, and over the fowl of the air, and over every living thing that moveth upon the earth" (Genesis 1:28). "And God blessed Noah and his sons, and said unto them, Be fruitful, and multiply, and replenish the earth" (Genesis 9:1).

According to Scripture, the greatest privilege given to man is to be a father and the greatest privilege of a woman is to be a mother. Anything short of this, unless denied this privilege by nature, is to make of those sacred intimacies of wedded life nothing more or less than licensed prostitution. I am fully aware that this is a serious charge to bring against those who are persistently and deliberately in rebellion against

God's primal commands, and it is a very unpopular teaching for this wicked generation, but so long as I have God's Word at hand to back me up in my statements, I have no fear of man's opinions. "For do I now persuade men, or God? Or do I seek to please men? for if I yet pleased men, I should not be the servant of Christ" (Galatians 1:10).

In no respect are the differences in man and woman more marked than in love. This is not only true in degree, but in kind. Love is the very nature of every normal woman, and in the last analysis, all her passions culminate in her maternal function. Her instincts from earliest childhood are all in that general direction. Therefore every little girl is a potential mother in embryo. She manifests this in her touching devotion to her dolls, which to her are as much alive as she is to her mother. As soon as she is old enough to hold a toy, she wants a doll, and would rather play "mother" than any other game. As the girl grows older, as witnessed in the case of our daughters, this instinct is manifested in her care for her own younger sisters and brothers. All these things are but the outward evidences of potential motherhood, and through proper instruction, every girl should be led to see these things, not as something low and vulgar and to be spoken of only in whispered jest, but as God's greatest gift for the perpetuation of the human race.

While woman plays the more important sexual role in that she conceives, gives birth to, and rears the child, the mothers should be just as careful to instill these same high and noble conceptions of the sexual instinct into the mind and heart of her sons. The mother has a responsibility here as well as the father, and especially in those tender years of childhood, and before the child's mind has been defiled concerning these things by his contacts with older boys. Every normal boy, as he reaches the age of puberty, begins to manifest unmistakable evidences of sexual longings and desires, consequently it becomes the duty of the parents to give him a right understanding of these things. He should be made to understand that his sexual power, if properly subjugated, is capable of lifting him to the highest possible attainments; but if given license it will sink him to the lowest depths of infamy.

At the age of puberty the boy grows rapidly, his voice breaks, signs of mustache appear, he seems embarrassed by the presence of others. He begins to manifest more politeness toward women, and becomes more interested in girls. He is becoming a man, and if there is ever a time when a boy needs a parent's kindness and sympathy, it is when he is between twelve and sixteen. But alas! far too often, when these inner forces and impulses are awakening and he finds himself stirred with strange emotions, he does not understand himself, neither do his friends seem to understand him. Sometimes even the parents are found nagging, teasing or making fun of him. Not having been taught the meaning of these new impulses, and because of a lack of parental sympathy, he does not find home a happy place, and very frequently he leaves it and seeks more sympathetic companionship elsewhere.

Therefore, as we have seen how that every little girl is a mother in embryo, we should be made to understand that every boy is a potential father in embryo. As he grows up into normal young manhood he most naturally seeks the companionship of some one of the opposite sex. He can't help it, for that is in perfect accord and keeping with his God-given instinct. I am giving in his own words, an incident related by Rev. William C. Boone, of Tennessee, that well illustrates the point I am trying to make. It is the story of a boy whose father was left a widower while the son was but an infant. For some reason his father became embittered toward the opposite sex. He took his young son out into an isolated section of the country, apart from all human associations, and reared him there in the solitudes of nature.

Until the son was nearly grown he had never been to a city or town, had never met another human being but his father. Then one day the father decided to take his son to the city and show him some of the wonders of civilization. They went down from their mountain home to the busy city, and spent the day looking at the sights. As they walked along they passed a group of girls. The son, who had never seen a girl before, was much interested. He asked his father what they were. He answered, "Oh, just a bunch of geese, my son!" That night when they were back in their lonely cabin in the wilds, the father asked the son what he had rather have than anything else of all he had seen on that memorable day. Without a moment's hesitation, the young man replied, "One of those geese!" Why of course he would. His father might keep him in ignorance respecting the opposite sex, but he could not destroy that innate sex impulse which is just as natural to every normal man and woman as life itself.

However, and in spite of these facts, we find that the average young person is permitted to grow up and enter into wedlock totally ignorant of its real significance. Many a mother is unwilling to teach her daughter the facts of sex, and yet quite willing that she should flirt with every Tom, Dick, and Harry who may be willing to take her to the dance or some other place of questionable amusement, hoping that she may be lucky (?) enough to capture one of these youngs bloods for a husband. Alas, how sad that the average girl should be permitted to grow up and enter wedlock totally ignorant of its divine purpose in perpetuating the human race through procreation. As one prominent writer said: "In the minds of many girls the wedding means only the public show, the display of elegant toilettes, the reception of costly gifts; and the preparation of marriage means too often merely the making of an elegant display. People generally do not ask concerning the fitness of the young people to enter on the solemn duties of life—do not ask how well they have been instructed concerning that which is before them; but the questions are all about clothes and gifts and ceremonials."

A genuine woman looks forward to the possibilities of motherhood with glad anticipation, and the girl who marries without a willingness to accept this responsibility is sacrificing that which, if rightly borne, will bring her the hightest possible development. Because she is created to love and be loved, she becomes a wife, a queen of her own home. Later she sacrifices her rounds of pleasure and walks with careful step, because of the unborn child which is concealed and nestles under a heart filled with a mother's love. How different it would be for every girl, no matter what her station in life may be, if she were thoroughly instructed and given a clear understanding of the sex relations and the privileges and responsibilities of wedlock. But in spite of the nobility of motherhood, we find that a large majority of young women in these days come to the marriage altar far better informed in methods of preventing conception, or in producing an abortion in case conception should take place, than they are in how to rear and take care of a family of children.

Reserve upon the subject of prospective motherhood, between a mother and her daughter, is silly, unwomanly and wholly unscriptural. God tells us in His Word, "Lo, children are an heritage of the Lord: and the fruit of the womb is his reward" (Psalm 127: 3). Paul, speaking under the inspiration of the Holy Spirit, said, "I will therefore that the younger women marry, bear children, guide the house, give none occasion to the adversary to speak reproachfully. For some are already turned aside after Satan" (I Timothy 5:14, 15). Because of these, and many other plain statements of Scripture, a Hebrew wife felt that the greatest dishonor that could befall her was to be childless. However, we find that conditions in so-called civilized social life have been reversed in these days, and it would seem as if the majority of our society women feel that the greatest curse that could come upon them would be for them to fulfill God's purpose for their lives and that they should conceive and bear children. We see that, "Motherhood is not a remote contingency, but the common duty and the common glory of womanhood. It is natural for wives to bear children, and unnatural, dangerous and sinful for them to evade this God-given function."

God's command in the beginning was, "Be fruitful

and multiply," and nowhere in Scripture do we find that this command has been revoked. Certainly God always commands that which is best for us, and the greatest happiness comes through obeying His will. However, in recent years we find many who are determined not to obey God's laws respecting the consequences of wedlock, and they are resorting to various methods of so-called birth control, which are an abomination in His sight. One of these plans is Onanism, which is not only detrimental to the health and well-being of both husband and wife, but so displeasing to God that He slew Onan who first practiced it (Genesis 38:9, 10). As one great Christian physician has said: "God has shown His great displeasure against every method practiced for thwarting His plans in preventing conception, and He will not permit these sins to go unpunished. . . . Ask the physician who has had large experience and he will tell you that those who disobey God's law to 'be fruitful and multiply' suffer the penalty of their crime, and so they can be found everywhere with sunken eyes, pale faces, sad hearts and unhappy lives. God created them male and female for a most sacred purpose, and they who trifle with these divine purposes will some day realize it is the greatest mistake of their life."

Another Christian physician, a teacher in a medical college, made the following strong pronouncement concerning this iniquitous business in his book entitled, "Sexology": "There is but one legitimate method of avoiding increase of family, and this should be adopted only for legitimate reasons, such as bona fide considerations of health or clearly established peculiarities of constitution. No sordid calculations of economy should have a feather's weight in its adoption. Whom the Lord endows with existence He provides for, according to the needs of His children, and no mere human fore-sight can discover whether economy lies in the increase or diminution in the number of children. This most judicious method of avoiding offspring is entire continence during the time it is desirable or necessary to remain exempt. All other methods of prevention of offspring are disgusting, beastly, positively wicked, as well as unnatural, and physically injurious. Some of them are so revolting that it is impossible to imagine how persons with the least pretension to decency can adopt them. Any deliberate preparations with such an object savor too much of cold-blooded calculation to be even possible with pure-minded people." In speaking of the use of contraception, Dr. Victor C. Pederson said, "It is concubinage, not marriage; the new era of prostitution, teaching our mothers and daughters, sweet-hearts and wives the common practices of the brothel. There is nothing in this birth control movement which the common prostitute does not practice in one way or another."

This leads me to go a step further and say a few words about another terrible evil which is being pal-liated and excused in our day to the extent that many high school girls are already introduced into its mys-teries, that is, infanticide—usually referred to as abor-tion. Outside the medical profession, very few indeed realize the prevalence of this crime, especially in so-called "high society." Despite everything which law and the church have been able to do in the last fifty or a hundred years, the number of illegal abortions annually has increased to an appalling degree. It is conservatively estimated that in the United States two million "illegal operations" are performed annually. Scores of thousands of women are being sent to premature graves through this crime. One doctor reports that out of thirty-four cases which came under his observation, twenty-two were followed by death. Another doctor reported that out of one hundred sixty cases, sixty were followed by death. Dr. Rheinhart, formerly Assistant Coroner's Physician, of Chicago, is reported in the daily press as having stated that 38,000 criminal operations are performed annually in that city. Miss Crowell, in *Charity and Commons*, says she has been informed that over 100,000 criminal operations are performed in New York annually. During a revival campaign in a western city of 6,000 population, I learned that eight women—most of them so-called society women—lost their lives through illegal operations in a single year.

It makes one shudder to think of these horrible consequences, yet as Rev. Brevard D. Sinclair said: "Here is a sin of such delicacy that people affect to be shocked when it is alluded to, and yet a sin which is practiced, applauded and commended so widely in private, that even the children are not ignorant of its prevalence among their elders. Indeed, a sin in which, in many cases, daughters are deliberately nurtured and trained, so that when opportunity is presented for its practice the conscience is so stultified and suborned by long training and familiarity with its hellish and poisonous consequences, that it is committed without compunction. The sin is none the less heinous, and the crime none the less wicked when it is performed by those who affect the best society, or who with unworthy

hands take the bread and wine at the communion table
of a dying Lord, who pronounced His blessing on the
pure in heart."

Has it never occurred to you that since the creation
of Adam and Eve there has never been a single break
in the thread of life that extends from that day down
to you and me?   It would have certainly been unfortunate for us had there been a single break for we
would never have been born. How it startles us to think
that we might never have been born at all.   When you
assume the responsibility of procreation you are taking your place in the long chain of life that has continued from the beginning and will go on and on producing other lives until the end of time.   But if you
refuse to take your place in this long chain of life, the
branch that leads to you comes to an end forever.
A line of descendants that might have become famous
the world over will never be brought into existence
because you have broken the chain.   Suppose Mrs.
Susanna Wesley had taken that attitude before the
birth of John, her fifteenth child, we would never have
heard of her or the Methodist churches that have been
blessed to millions of people during the last two centuries.

Some who are always trying to find an excuse for
their sins will say there is no harm so long as there is
no life, that is, the so-called "quickening."   But there
is life just as soon as conception takes place.   If there
is no life why try to kill the child?   When an untaught
wife, and a young husband whose conscience has been
seared by sin, go to a doctor and proceed to tell him
that they do not want children so early in their married life; that they want to enjoy themselves for a

while, or take a trip to Europe, and then ask the doctor to help them out by destroying their unborn child—they are at heart and in the sight of God already guilty of murder (I John 3:15). At the Great Judgment the Lord will certainly ask them one terrible question: "Where are those children that I gave you, and you murdered them before they were born?" For let it be remembered once for all, that when the husband encourages or insists upon this illegal act, he is as guilty of murder as the doctor or his wife.

There is, in fact, no time after conception when it can be said that the child has not life, and the crime of destroying human life is as heinous and as sure before the period of "quickening" as afterward—the sin in all cases is the same. Murder is the intent of the heart and not in the act alone. You have committed murder as surely as if the dead child lay in your arms. The husband is a partner with the wife in her guilt and responsibility, and all the oceans in the world cannot cleanse him from blood-guiltiness, and their so-called expediency may be answered from God's Word, "the wages of sin is death." Our sympathy for the girl seduced outside wedlock, and who is bordering upon insanity because of her burden of shame, is great; but for the man who refuses to marry the girl he has betrayed and drives her to the greater guilt and danger of murdering her unborn child, it is well that a merciful God will be his judge as to the final consequences. Hear His word of warning, "But the fearful, and unbelieving, and the abominable, and murderers, and whoremongers, and sorcerers, and idolaters, and all liars, shall have their part in the lake which burneth with fire and brimstone: which is the second death" (Rev. 21:8).

A physician in one of the cities where we were engaged in a union revival campaign, sent me an account of an incident that may help us to locate the responsibility for this dastardly deed. A mother stepped into the doctor's office carrying a bright and beautiful baby a year old. Seating herself near the doctor, who was her family physician, she said, "Doctor, I want you to help me out of trouble. My baby is only one year old, and I have conceived again, and I do not want to have children so close together." "What do you expect me to do?" asked the physician. "Oh, anything to get rid of it for me," she replied. After thinking seriously for a moment the doctor said, "I think I can suggest a better method of helping you out. If you object to two children so near together, the best way would be to kill the one on your lap and let the other one come on. It is very easy to get at the one on your lap, and it makes no difference to me which one I kill for you. Besides, it might be dangerous for you if I undertook to kill the younger one." As the doctor finished he reached for a hatchet which was used to cut kindling, and continued by asking the mother to lay the baby out on her lap, and turn her head the other way. The woman almost fainted away as she jumped from her chair and uttered just one word, "murderer!" A few words of explanation from the doctor soon convinced the woman that his offer to commit murder was no worse than her request for the destruction of the unborn child. In either case it would be murder, the only difference would be in the age of the victim.

That results of this criminal act are often immediately fatal to the mother, is indicated by the press which teems with the reports of such cases almost daily. It is true, as Mr. Sinclair says, "Many a woman is buried with Christian burial, over whose grave ought to be placed a tombstone with this inscription: 'Here lies a suicide, assisted to her grave by her murderers—her husband, her female counsellors, and a conscienceless physician.'" In addition to this, it is the universal testimony of physicians, that even though the mother survives the shock of this terrible outrage against God and nature, she is doomed to a life of suffering and misery; physically, mentally and morally. "The risk of infection is approximately ten times greater than at ordinary child birth for the reason that the uterine cavity must be invaded, while in child birth this is rarely the case. Also for every woman who dies as a result of abortion, several are disabled, sometimes permanently, or rendered sterile, or at subsequent pregnancy, suffer from the after effects of abortion."

Then suppose the attempt against the child does not succeed, as is very often the case, what fearful results may follow! No doubt but that the murderous intent of the mother will be stamped indelibly upon the character of the unwelcome child, giving to it a natural propensity for the commission of crime. The fact was brought out in the trial of Guiteau, the murderer of President James A. Garfield, that for several months before he was born, his mother tried by the use of drugs and other means, to destroy the life of her unborn child, but was unsuccessful. In other words, Guiteau was born with a propensity for crime, and the responsibility for the murder of President Garfield was traceable to the mother who had endeavored to destroy the life of her unborn child.

The increase in crime in the United States is out of all proportion to the increase in population; the increase being five hundred per cent in thirty years. It is believed by many of our best authorities that the maternal impressions will be found a prime factor in the cause of an individual's criminal actions. The question, "Why are there so many criminals who are seemingly unable to refrain from criminal acts?" is a subject that has received far too little attention. In my judgment, after these years of study and meditation upon the subject, this increase of crime is not due to environment or the faulty education of the individual, so much as upon the innate tendencies and desires to commit criminal acts because of wrong maternal impressions. Professor T. W. Shannon, an evangelist, relates the following incident that was given to him by an aged physician which is a fair illustration of this principle.

The physician told that when he was a young doctor, a father called him to his home to see some sick member of the family. While he was diagnosing the case and preparing the remedies, he noticed the little girl caressing her father, and a son some two years older was viciously tearing off the heads of his sister's paper dolls. A little later the pet cat of the house entered the room, and seeing the cruel boy, ran under the bed. The boy dropped the dolls, ran to the wood box, seized a long splinter, crawled under the bed, dragged out the cat, holding the cat to the floor with his left hand and with his right hand holding the splinter he tried to saw off the cat's head. Soon the dog entered and he caught him and tried to saw his head off. When his services were over, the father followed him to the front gate and said, "Doctor, did you observe the difference between my two children?" "Yes," was my reply, "What caused the difference in the dispositions of the children?" "My little girl was wanted in our home and the boy was not," was the father's sad reply. Then the doctor added, "I lived to see that boy become a criminal." Yes, in fact he was born as a criminal—his heart being filled with hate.

Probably no drug or other material means was used in this case. It was the effect of a criminal state of mind on the part of the mother; the father, according to his own admission, being a party thereto. When drugs or other material means are used the results are often worse, if that be possible, that is, a brain disorder that results in confronting the guilty parents with an epileptic or feeble-minded child. The predisposing cause of epilepsy is admitted to be a brain disorder which is due in many cases to an attempted and unsuccessful destruction of the unborn child by the use of more or less powerful drugs. The feeble-minded have increased in this country more than five hundred per cent in the last sixty years. It is estimated that no less than thirty-two per cent of the more than 300,000 epileptic and idiotic persons in the United States have been caused by poisonous drugs used to prevent conception and in an attempted abortion. This means then that 96,000 of these unfortunates have been produced by a wilful violation of nature's laws. But after all, even this represents but a small fraction of the evil effects, for hundreds of thousands have been still-born from this cause, or born weaklings, only to eke out a miserable existence or fill a premature grave.

I am fully aware that I have given considerable space to the discussion of this unpleasant subject, but it has been because I hope to be able to impress parents with the fact that the special destiny of a husband is to be a father and that of a woman is to be a wife and a mother, and that you could not bring any greater dishonor to yourselves than to rebel against God's plan for your destiny. Then, too, I hope I may succeed in saving the lives of many more unborn children who will be a joy and a source of comfort and blessing to their parents later in life. Many such cases have been revealed to me following our special services for "men only" and "women only," and as illustrating this point I am quoting in full a letter received from a lady in Minneapolis, entitled, "A True Story by a Saved Daughter":

"I was one of seven healthy children born to poor, but honest parents, living a few miles from Minneapolis. I had been married about two years when my mother came to see me, being greatly agitated because she was to become a mother again. Feeling that she had enough children she wanted me to tell her where to go that she might get rid of this one. I told my mother I did not know of any such place, and I told her that I was afraid she would be taken away from us children. I urged her to have one more and live for all of us. I was unsaved at the time and did not know how to deal with my mother, so she went away very much discouraged. The days slipped by, till one day the news came that we had a new fine healthy baby brother. He is now twenty-five years old and seems to be my mother's favorite child. He has a fine way with her, taking care of her, and she seems to enjoy his companionship more than any other child she has. So the baby that at first was not wanted is a wonderful son and a great comfort and support to her in her old age, and as the old saying runs, he is 'the apple of her eye'."

On an average, at least four children must be born and grow to maturity in every American home in our land to prevent the native American race from dying out. It is a notorious fact, sad to say, that on an average the families of native Americans are so small that the children hardly replace the parents. It is not an uncommon thing too, for many of our so-called society women to make their boast that they know too much to have children. Often these knowing ones may be seen leading around a solitary little one whose brothers and sisters have all been nipped in the bud and destroyed by the cruel hand of the abortionist. These thoughts are not pleasant, I know—they are horrible. But in spite of this fact we find in what is called "good society" very few, even among professing Christian men and women, who have any proper Scriptural ideas on this subject.

Marriage was ordained of God and is for home and children, and unless young people are prepared to make the home and to desire children, they commit a grievous sin to enter its sacred portals. Make it clear to every daughter in our land that for them to enter marriage with any other thought than that they will be the joyful mothers of children, they commit a grievous sin against God and nature. As I have said, undoubtedly the special destiny of woman is to be a wife and a mother. If, from causes for which they are not responsible, they fail of this destiny, there are on every hand, the poor and motherless, the forsaken and down-trodden, the sinful and the sorrowful —behold your charge! Some of these may become your spiritual children, who would rise up in the day of Christ's glorious coming again to call you blessed forever and ever. "He maketh the barren woman to keep house, and to be a joyful mother of children. Praise ye the Lord" (Psalm 113:9).

CHAPTER VII.

HEREDITY AND PRENATAL CULTURE

I FEEL that the time has past when ignorance concerning the divine laws of heredity is excusable on the part of any one with an average intelligence. All farmers and stock-men, whether they have had the advantages of a college education or not, are well acquainted with the facts, laws and principles of heredity when applied to plant and animal life. What reason is there then for all the prudery and the vast amount of false modesty that surrounds the whole subject of procreation when applied to the human family. I am certain that every right-thinking prospective parent must be anxious to bring into the world and rear just the best and brightest children possible. But to be able to do this both parents must be in harmony with those divine laws of heredity and prenatal culture.

Many of my readers may feel that it is too late to prevent the mistakes of their own lives respecting their families, therefore, why bother about the subject now? But what about your own children and your children's children? Is it not high time for you to cast aside that false modesty of yours and begin at once the task of thoroughly informing your children lest they fall into similar mistakes and more serious blunders? If you are in doubt as to your responsibility to your own children, I should suggest that you visit

111

some of our prisons, reformatories, poorhouses, idiot and insane asylums and inquire into the history of those poor unfortunate creatures. You will be surprised to find that the large majority of those unfortunates are in their present miserable plight because of the sins and ignorance of their parents. In those places you will find the sins of the parents duplicated in their unfortunate descendants, practically all of which might have been precluded through obedience to the divine laws of heredity and prenatal culture.

I am fully aware that it is too late now to put an end to the miseries, sorrows and woes of those unfortunate creatures—death alone can avail for that in the majority of such cases — but what about your children's children? Are you going to educate and instruct them along all other lines and leave them in ignorance of the laws of God respecting procreation? In my ministeries which have taken me from one end of this land to the other time and again, I have observed many of these unfortunate cases in the homes of parents who were considered normal, cultured and supposedly well educated. But because of their ignorance of the laws of God respecting procreation they have brought into the world a child who will be a source of shame and embarrassment to the parents so long as they live.

Some parents seem to be laboring under the false assumption that God was cruel and unjust in establishing the law of heredity and thus compelling innocent children to suffer because of the sins of their guilty parents. But in my endeavor to disabuse your mind of this unjust charge against our God and Heavenly Father, I would first remind you that this law was made—as we learn from the first chapter of Genesis —before man was created and later fell into sin. It is a universal law of cause and effect and God could no more change it without bringing all creation into a state of chaos and confusion than he could reverse or change the law of gravitation. Then in the second place, I would call your attention to the fact that "God is love," therefore every act of His respecting the human race from the time of creation down to the present moment has been prompted by His unbounded spirit of benevolence and love.

Isn't it strange that parents will proudly claim every perfection of a child as an inherited quality, but if there should be a defective child born into the home as a result of parental sin and misconduct, they immediately blame the divine law of heredity. We must remember that God is a God of justice as well as a God of mercy, and while all His laws were made with our welfare in mind, if we in ignorance or deliberate willfulness violate them we will certainly suffer the consequences by bringing into the world defective children. There are two things which are absolutely inseparable—sin and suffering. Therefore, this law is not a punishment from God upon innocent, helpless children, for He is in no sense responsible for such suffering. The parents themselves, who in their early life thought they could do as they pleased and sowed their wild oats, are wholly to blame for this vast section of unfortunate suffering humanity. It is wholly a matter of cause and effect and if people will not abide by the laws of God they must expect to suffer the consequences of their sins in their own children. "But if ye will not do so, behold, ye have sinned against the Lord: and be sure your sin will find you out" (Numbers 32:23). And there is no place on earth where your sins are more sure to find you out than in your own children.

Some seem to be under the impression that heredity and prenatal culture are one and the same thing—but such is not the case. While these two principles are closely related, yet in their final analysis there is an essential difference. After considerable study and observation, I am persuaded that the husband influences the child more definitely through the transmission of his ancestral hereditary characteristics and tendencies; while the mother transmits to the child particular qualities and characteristics by and through her state of mind and conduct during the time the child is being formed in her body. I believe these two things are taught in the Scripture— the first through plain doctrinal statements, and the other is illustrated in the lives and experiences of certain Bible characters.

We find the law of heredity recorded in the first chapter of Genesis, where it is plainly stated that every plant and animal should bring forth after its kind. We are so accustomed to seeing the outworking of this law that most people give it little or no thought. In the second command of the decalogue we find both the law and the gospel of heredity set forth in contrast: "I the Lord thy God am a jealous God, visiting the iniquity of the fathers upon the children unto the third and fourth generation of them that hate me; and shewing mercy unto thousands of them that love me, and keep my commandments" (Exodus 20:5-6).

It has been said that all great men had great mothers. This is true, no doubt, largely because of

the fact that mothers have a greater opportunity to influence and determine the characteristics of the child
through prenatal influences than the father has through
heredity in the initial act of begetting the child. This
makes possible the Gospel side of heredity as illustrated in the case of Hannah, who through her earnest
prayer and yearning for her son caused Samuel to be
well-born. He was earnestly desired and sought after
as a gift from God, for every Hebrew wife felt that
no greater calamity could befall her than that she
should be childless. However, but little could be said of
Hannah's husband, except that he was a devout man and
faithful in his attendance at the various annual feasts,
and in his outward and formal worship of Jehovah.
No doubt he contributed much toward the religious instincts of his famous son, but he had other children
by another wife and no mention is made of them as
having distinguished themselves in any way as being
above the average children of that day and time. Therefore, we must conclude that Samuel—as well as the majority of those who have achieved those things in life
which differentiated them from other men of their times
—owed their greatness to their mothers rather than
to their fathers. In fact history shows this to be true
—three to one—in favor of mother.

To cover the whole scope of the law of heredity
in a single chapter would be out of the question in a
book the size I have in mind for this one. I trust, however, that the facts and illustrations here given may
lead to a further study of the subject on the part of
prospective parents, who are anxious to do the best
possible for their children yet to be. After giving two
striking illustrations of the divine principles of hered-

ity, we will give further consideration to the more practical and immediate subject of prenatal culture— that which all intelligent prospective parents can work out more or less in detail for themselves. Parenthood is not a remote contingency, but the duty and the common glory of every well sexed married couple. If for some unknown reason children are not born to healthy parents they should certainly adopt two or more from among the multitude of homeless little ones and give them the best possible environment.

First, I wish to call attention to the fact that a genius for vice or crime is a matter of inheritance as much as that of a taste for music, art or mechanics. History proves that these abnormal instincts run through many families. The reader is doubtless more or less familiar with the records of the Max Jukes family of New York State, for these facts and figures have found their way into print and have been used often in illustrating the dark side of the law of heredity. He was born in 1720. Of his 903 descendants that have been traced, 300 children died prematurely; 200 were thieves; 145 drunkards; 90 were prostitutes; 91 illegitimate children; while 480 out of the 903 were suffering from venereal diseases. Of the 200 who were criminally inclined, three paid the death penalty and over 100 were imprisoned on an average of thirteen years each. It is said that the various members of this family cost the State of New York more than a million dollars.

In contrast to this terrible record, I now direct your attention to the Jonathan Edwards family which furnishes a splendid illustration of the gospel side of heredity. He was born in 1703. Of the 1394 of his descendants whose records were studied, it was learned that 13 were presidents of leading universities and colleges, 65 were college and university professors, 60 were doctors, 100 were ministers, 60 were prominent authors, 100 were lawyers and 30 were judges. A number were senators, congressmen, mayors of cities and ministers of foreign countries. We are told that so far as known, only one of this famous family ever left a blot upon the family record and that was Aaron Burr who fought a duel and killed a fellow citizen.

In my travels I have met a number of the descendants of the Edwards family and without exception, so far as I have been able to learn, they were upright, honorable citizens, most of them living the Christian life. I have never met anyone who claimed to be a descendant of the Jukes family. In fact I would consider it to be doubtful if one could be found. As we have learned already, God declares that He visits the iniquities of the fathers upon the children unto the third and fourth generations of those that hate Him, and in His infinite mercy and love for the unborn millions who would be blighted by degeneracy and suffering, He has ordained that there shall be no fifth generation born of these degenerates. Had not God established such a law when He reduced the longevity of man from several hundred years to three score and ten, this old world would have long since been filled with violence such as prevailed before the flood when "God saw that the wickedness of man was great in the earth, and every imagination of the thoughts of his heart was only evil continually" (Genesis 6: 5).

I might call attention to many illustrations of the twofold principal of heredity—but these must suffice for the present. Max Jukes was an idle, thriftless hunter, a hard drinker and licentious, who married into a family of five sisters, several of whom were illegitimate and three of whom were known to be unchaste— hence the terrible record of crime and vileness until they went out of existence in the third and fourth generations. Jonathan Edwards and his wife were both well born, and were converted in childhood—Dr. Edwards being converted at the age of seven. They were both refined and well educated, insisting upon the strictest family discipline in the rearing of their own children, and they became a striking illustration of the fulfillment of the last sentence of the second command, "And showing mercy unto thousands of them (that is, generations) that love me, and keep my commandments," therefore their generations are still in evidence and will go on until the end of time.

Many have overlooked the fact that the expression "thousands of them that love me" does not mean thousands of individuals, but thousands of "generations." Therefore, since the degenerates end with the third and fourth generation—being unable to reproduce themselves—it must be true that if they would trace their ancesters back a few generations they would find that they came originally from a good and honorable ancestry. Or, as another has expressed it, "Just to the extent that man has received a good or a bad heredity, keeps or violates law, accepts or rejects the grace of God, just to that extent does he recover or degenerate, create a good or a bad environment, and will transmit a good or a bad heredity to his posterity."

We believe that in the law and the gospel of heredity and prenatal culture, of the two parents, the mother has a far greater opportunity for determining the special characteristics of the child than the father. While the father at the time of the initial of life is contributing that which is "bone of his bone, flesh of his flesh," and that which will reveal certain of his characteristics, yet what the child shall be in character and ability will be determined very largely by the mental, moral and spiritual state of the mother while the blood from her heart is flowing through the veins of the child. "For the life of the flesh is in the blood: and I have given it to you upon the altar to make atonement for your souls: for it is the blood that maketh atonement by reason of the life" (Leviticus 17: 11).

Note the expression: "the life of the flesh is in the blood." At the initial of life a new being is begotten which is the sum total of the physical, mental and spiritual life extending back to Adam. The procreative cells of both male and female are in the blood which furnishes life for every cell of our being. Therefore why should it be thought strange that the condition of the blood should have such a decided effect upon the physical, mental and moral or spiritual nature of this newly begotten soul during the nine months before it makes its visible appearance at birth? It is a well known scientific fact that the mental state of an individual affects the various secretions of the body for good or evil. Many cases are on record where mothers have nursed a tiny babe after being in a rage of anger and thereby thrown the child into convulsions. If such a thing can happen after a child is born, what might not a mother accomplish in the three-fold nature of her unborn child while her own life blood is coursing through its veins, carrying with it the effects of her various moods and thoughts of good or evil. Envy, hate and jealousy will disturb the organs of digestion and later these emotions are visible in the face of the one who harbors them, showing the power of the mind and emotions over the physical.

"From these facts we see that the mother has the advantage of the father in influencing the forming body, the plastic brain and the sensitive soul of the child. Owing to the double standard of morals it is certainly a blessing to the world that this is true. Whatever is undesirable in the father, especially in his moral life, in a measure may be overcome by the mother. The mother's physical, mental and moral life is in her blood." That the conduct of the mother can and does affect the child, even to the changing of the facial expression as well as the mental and moral nature has been illustrated time and again. The mother may not have beauty of face and form, but she has power to bestow grace and beauty to her child.

In the *Review of Reviews,* for November, 1892, is a sketch of Mrs. Willard, the mother of one of the world's best known Christian reformers, the late Frances E. Willard, in which it is stated, "That previous to the birth of Frances, Mrs. Willard often attended a singing school which was held near her home, and that she was attracted by the features and brown hair of a young woman who was a regular attendant." The features and hair as well as the moral character of that young woman were reproduced in Frances E. Willard, whom the humanitarian element of society everywhere delights to honor and admire.

In a Missouri town a mother invited Professor T. W. Shannon, whom I have quoted in the second paragraph above, into her husband's store and related her experiment in prenatal culture. From her earliest teens she had entertained a wish that should she ever become a mother, her child might have golden hair. When she discovered that she was to be a mother she asked her husband to get her two pictures—one to be the picture of a perfect boy, the other, the picture of a perfect girl, each to have golden hair. While in St. Louis, purchasing a stock of goods, he secured the pictures desired. She placed them in her room where she could frequently see and admire them. After calling Mr. Shannon's attention to the dark hair of her husband and her own dark hair, she proudly introduced the golden haired boy, then five years of age.

Some time ago I came across an interesting account of an entire family of artists influenced in this direction by the efforts of intelligent parents. I give it word for word as published in a Chicago paper. The family of artists consists of father and eight children, many of them noted in art circles. In speaking on the subject, the father, Mr. Betts, says: "All my life I have been interested in the subject of prenatal influence. My wife has shared my interest, and our ideas on the subject have always been in harmony. Mrs. Betts is not an artist, but she is a woman of artistic temperament, and I have always considered her my best critic.

Before the birth of the oldest son I visited with my wife the best art gallaries. She looked upon masterpieces of all ages and took up a course of art studies. She became genuinely and intensely interested. I am sure that this has resulted in making our son an artist who surpasses me in ability. She pursued the same course of study prior to the birth of each of our children. Before Grace was born my wife began studying music as well as painting, and our daughter has astonished thousands by her skill with the violin, although she never took a music lesson." Mr. Betts closed his remarks by saying, "I believe the possibilities of prenatal influence are unlimited."

The mother can do much to influence the appearance and mental and moral states of the unfolding life. This has been proved over and over again. The prospective mother should think beautiful thoughts, should surround herself with lovely pictures and some heavy reading matter that will lead to deep thinking, study and concentration of the mind. Her heart should warm with gladness and joyful anticipation as she meditates upon the possible future achievements and accomplishments of the little one there nestling just beneath her heart of love and affection. Of course the husband must share this intense interest along with the wife by providing for her comfort and in helping to create an environment of light and joyful anticipation. If the very best results are to be accomplished, this should be a time of restraint and continency on his part.

Many a poet or preacher has been born of parents whose lives were poems and sermons of peace and joy, but who were never able to express a couplet in rhyme or make a public speech. Susanna Wesley, with the song of praise and the gospel of peace in her heart, gave to the world two sons whose spiritual achievements in song and sermon have carried peace to millions of souls. She was no preacher, but lived the song and sermon which found expression in her sons. The young wife may not have a powerful intellect but she may bestow one on her children; she may not have great beauty herself, but she can certainly make her children beautiful both in person and character.

"What do you expect to do when you get to America?" asked a fellow passenger of a woman who was crossing the Atlantic Ocean a century and a half ago. "Do? Why raise governors for them." Well, her aspirations and visions were fulfilled in a very definite manner, for she became the mother of General John Sullivan of New Hampshire, and James Sullivan, Governor of Massachusetts. This young woman thought cream, and transmitted cream, and I would say to all young women, you think skimmed milk and you will transmit skimmed milk. Because of your wrong impressions of sex-life, girls may chafe under the suggestion of children yet unborn, but let me say to any young woman that may be reading these lines, that what your children may become depends upon two things: first, upon that which you are building into your physical and moral character; and, then, the impressions you make upon them before birth through prenatal culture. Training and environment may help to overcome the bad hereditary tendencies, and of course the grace of God is sufficient in the salvation of all classes, but you can never do through training and environment what you might have accomplished through prenatal culture.

In the "Life and Work of Henry Ward Beecher," by Thomas W. Knox, we are told how the love of flowers was inherited by Dr. Beecher from his mother, who, just before he was born, spent much time amid the flowers about their homestead. She was constantly exchanging flower seeds and slips of shrubs. In the midst of his busy life as one of the greatest preachers of his day, he wrote a book on flower culture because of his great interest in the subject. Beecher's father was a scholarly preacher, and we are told that his mother spent much time in pondering over the works of the great thinkers of that time. With the splendid hereditary influence through the father and mother with a heart of true devotion to the interests of her unborn child, is it particularly remarkable that they were used of God to give our country just the man we needed in the time of our nation's greatest crisis—the Civil War?

The ancient Romans certainly believed in the force of prenatal culture. They insisted that prospective mothers be surrounded with examples of courage, heroism, strength and purity and that they refrain from wine and liquors of all kinds. Naturally enough, these influences were transmitted by the mother to her children and thus the mothers greatly aided in making Rome the mistress of the world in her day. It is said that the mother of Napoleon Bonaparte spent several months marching with her husband, sharing with him all the excitement, dangers and hardships of war just before the birth of her son. This, no doubt, had much to do with making Napoleon the greatest warrior of his day.

Why should crime have increased over four hundred per cent in our country during the last thirty years? Having studied these things for twenty-five years or more, I am convinced in my own mind that these conditions are very largely due to natural causes, that is, the frightful dissipation on the part of the majority of the mothers for the last two or three generations. The mania for money-making, cigarette smoking, cocktail drinking, movie-mad, dance-crazy and card-playing has so dominated the lives of our women generally, that no thoughtful person could have anticipated anything different from the conditions which confront us today everywhere throughout our nation. The mothers of our nation have sown to the wind and we are reaping the whirlwind. Society is made up of individuals, and the natural tendencies of each individual are very largely determined by the mother.

I can give space here to but one illustration of the effects of these various forms of dissipation. As far as possible I am relating it in the mother's own words: "My mother was a Christian; she taught us that it was wrong to play cards and dangerous to dance. She practiced what she taught and carefully warned me of all such perils. I married at an early age and forsook my Christian mother's example and wise counsel and followed the leadership of my husband, who was not a Christian.

"He taught me to play cards and took me to dances, and I became infatuated with both these forms of amusement. When at home, my husband and I would often sit at our card table until midnight, and if there was a dance within our reach we always went if it was possible to get there. By and by our first child came to our home, and I have reaped in him what I sowed on the dancing floor, at the card table and at the theatre. For I soon found that I had 'marked' my boy before he was born with special tendencies in the direction of evil associations and practices in which I had indulged to my heart's content.

"While but a mere child he became a proficient card-player. He was at home on the ball-room floor, and found his natural environment at these places. He became a professional gambler, and his short life ended in the paths in which I had set his feet. He came to the end of his life after a brief illness without warning from any person that death was near. He died as he had lived—without repentance toward God and without forgiveness of sins. He lived the life he learned from his mother before I was saved, and died without knowing the Saviour whom his mother had forgotten for a time and whom I now love, adore and serve. I have no doubt but what my son's soul is lost forever and I did it. After his death his body was sent home and we buried him in a Christless grave and thus ends the saddest experience that could ever come to a mother who had forgotten God."

In contrast to this dark picture, and as further evidence as to the tremendous influence which can be, and is exerted for good or bad by the mental, moral and spiritual condition of the prospective mother upon the character of the unborn child, I am sketching the experience of Mrs. D— of W——, as given by C. J. Bayer: "The father is an old and reliable merchant. Within the year of the birth of their third child, Mrs. D., at family prayers and upon retiring, would ask the Lord to so guide her footsteps, that she would educate one of her two living boys, at that time aged seven and twelve years, to become a minister of the Gospel. She earnestly desired that one of them should become a preacher of Christ and Him crucified. She gave the prospective child no thought on that line. Mr. D. says his wife was fully engrossed with the idea that one of her sons should become a preacher.

"The third child was a boy, very kind and loving in disposition, conscientious in the extreme. As a child he preferred stories of the Bible or such as were of a religious nature. As he became old enough to choose his own reading matter, it was noticed that he preferred the Bible. At this writing and at the age of eighteen years of age, this young man is preparing for the ministry. The oldest son, whom Mrs. D. wanted to make a preacher of, is a bookkeeper in a bank; the next son is connected with a mining company in Colorado."

The conclusion to which the Bible illustrations of Hannah, the mother of Samuel—and many others that might be cited—and from experience and observation of modern times, is that every thought of the prospective mother is registered, or impressed upon the body, brain and future character of the expected child. I know some of the so-called worldly-wise philosophers assert strongly that acquired characteristics are not transmitted; but I would rather accept the Bible and the experience of history any time, rather than the teachings of the so-called philosophers and scientists, for, as Professor Elmer Gates and others have demonstrated, their theories do not accord with the facts.

I might relate many cases from my experience and observation which forcibly illustrate both the dark and the bright side of heredity and prenatal influences. But space will not permit. However, I trust enough has been said to lead many prospective parents into a further investigation of this most interesting and important subject. I close with the following strong statement from a book by Dr. Dio Lewis, entitled "Chastity." He says:

"It is not carrying this subject too far to say that if any trade or profession seems particularly desirable, the genius for success in that line may be given to the child by proper effort before its birth. The mother whose mind persistently dwells upon any chosen subject during this nine months of gestation will surely see in her offspring the mark of her thoughts. Beauty of person, strength of mind, sweetness of disposition and holy aspiration may be assured to posterity by parents wise and loving enough to fulfill the laws which lead to the desired results."

CHAPTER VIII.

A VIRTUOUS WOMAN FINDING A GODLY HUSBAND

KING SOLOMON, who was inspired to write most of the book of Proverbs, said, "Whoso findeth a wife findeth a good thing, and obtaineth favor of the Lord" (Proverbs 18: 22). The woman being included in all the Scriptures in a generic sense, and since every truly virtuous young woman must make her choice of a husband from among the young swains that come seeking her favors, this passage might be rendered as follows: "Whoso findeth a husband findeth a good thing, and obtaineth favor of the Lord." But certainly no Christian young woman should expect to obtain the favor of the Lord if she deliberately chooses to accept the company of those known to be His enemies. Every truly God-approved marriage must be prompted by love, and how can a young woman truly love a man whom she knows to be an enemy of her Lord and Savior Jesus Christ? "Because the carnal mind is enmity against God: for it is not subject to the law of God, neither indeed can be" (Romans 8: 7).

If we are to judge by the divorce proceedings, and by what we observe of marital unhappiness as we pass along through life, it would seem that in a very large per cent of marriages, the contracting parties knew very little, if anything at all, about that thing we call love. Webster's Dictionary describes love as "An emotion, sentiment, or feeling of pleasurable attraction toward

or delight in a person or thing which induces a desire
for the presence, possession, well-being, or promotion
of its object; the strong yet tender longing for whatever
is considered most worthy of desire in any relation; a
strong feeling of affection for or devoted attachment to
a person; especially a feeling of intimate personal sympathy and affection toward an individual of the opposite sex."

I have quoted Webster's description of "love" quite
at length for I am fully convinced that the average
married couple has never read it. At least, so long
as we find that according to Government statistics, one
home out of every seven is being wrecked by divorce,
we should naturally conclude that the average husband
and wife have never known the meaning of love in
their experience of wedded life. According to our observations, it would seem that far too many young
couples were led to the marriage altar through a temporary infatuation—rather than love. Webster's syno-
nyms for "infatuation" are "folly, madness, intoxication, foolishness, unreason," which to my mind more
fitly describes a very large number of present day
marriages. Too many of them are prompted by lust
rather than by that holy and divine principle of love,
which when found will make the two truly "one flesh."

It is high time for our young people to stop looking
silly and embarrassed when they speak of love. There
is nothing silly about it, although some folk are silly
because they are in love. Love is the purest and most
noble of all God's gifts to men and women. True love
never degrades either man or woman. It never descends
to those coarse, vulgar familiarities which are called
by various names such as "petting," "necking," or as

formerly dubbed, "spooning." Familiarity breeds contempt, and there is no more dangerous thing in the world than for a young girl to be deceived into supposing that merely the awakening of the maternal or sexual instinct is an evidence of true love. To be able to love a person, one must find lovable qualities of mind and traits of character in the one loved. It is, therefore, an absolute impossibility for total strangers to fall in love at sight. It is quite possible for two young people to become infatuated at sight—but true love at first sight—never! I use the word love, of course, in its Scriptural meaning.

True love demands a single standard of morals and virtue for both parties. Let me ask that professing Christian young woman who is contemplating a hasty marriage, a few pointed questions. Do you love that young man because of his good heredity, free of a strain of insanity or some other abnormality? Do you love him because he is free from the taint of congenital venereal diseases, or some other physical or moral stigma? The young lady replies, "I do not know anything particular about his parents or his past." Then you do not know whether he is the son of a thief, an embezzler, a drunkard or a degenerate. Allow me to ask another question or two. Do you love him because of his personal qualities, physically, intellectually, morally and spiritually? Has that young man kept himself pure; has he high ideals, does he believe in the sanctity of the home; does he believe in living up to his marriage vows; has he been a rounder, a sport, a lustful, licentious, drunken blasphemer, a gambler or a rake? Does he know that since you are a Christian, your body is a temple of the Holy Spirit? To all these questions the young woman simply replies, "I really know nothing about him, but I know I love him anyway." Then, while I dislike to speak so plainly, I say you are a little sentimental fool, and have never come to know the first principles of true love.

If young women would be half as vehement and emphatic in their condemnation of fallen men as they are of fallen women, there would be an immediate moral revolution in this land of ours. Women are the best missionaries of the cause of Purity. Just let them make it known that they will refuse to marry men who fail to bring to the bridal chamber the same purity which men expect from womanhood, and it will start the greatest moral revolution since the Reformation. Six hundred girls and young women in Bristol, England, where one of the greatest tobacco businesses in the world is established, resolved to have nothing to do with the boys and young men who smoked. We are told that certain young men took it to heart and in a short time they had induced five hundred fifty boys and young men to pledge themselves not to smoke.

I could never understand why many Christian young women will permit young men to spend half of Saturday night in a saloon, or a gambling den, and the other half in a house of prostitution, then come around Sunday evening with a cigarette in their mouths and the smell of liquor on their breath and arm the girls off to church or some place of amusement. What incentive is there to live a clean life if the young men know that they can make beasts of themselves and yet keep company with some of the so-called best girls of the community? Yes, young women must be angels in their sight, but what about their standards in your sight?

Too many young women have accepted the prevalent idea that young men must "sow their wild oats," and they think if the lover reforms before marriage and remains true thereafter, that that is all they can reasonably demand. This proves to be a sad chapter in many a young woman's life. Just as a woman in a house of shame said, "We use the young men of this town until they are worthless, then the Christian women marry them." When young girls turn from clean, pure-blooded young men, with horny hands and sun-burned brows, caused by hard work, and marry some bejeweled, whiskey-soaked libertine who has plenty of money for a fine automobile and all kinds of sports—heaven weeps and hell hurrahs—for there is one more case for the operating table of the surgeon and the divorce courts!

The situation has become so serious because of the rapid increase of social diseases, I should say that twenty-five dollars or more spent by young women, who have no parents or proper guardians, in securing the services of an honorable detective to look up the record and investigate the character of the young man who proposes marriage, would not only prevent many broken hearts, but would save many a girl from an untimely death. If a young man believes in the purity and virtue of the young woman whom he asks to become his wife, why should she not have the privilege of asking him if he has retained his purity and chastity for the queen of his heart. If he has not, he insults the young woman when he asks her to trade her purity and honor for his impurity and his dishonor. Sad to say, there is not one thing in the law in this country which protects marriageable girls and women along this line. If a man murders your daughter or your sister in cold blood, he can be sent to the electric chair or to prison for life. If he is a moral degenerate and physically rotten because of his sin, he may deceive her into marriage and send her to her grave within six months or a year and nothing is said about it.

If girls were faithfully taught these things by their mothers, they would not only be careful how they marry immoral men, but it would seem to me as if they would shrink from personal contact with them as from a viper. The reformed prodigal son has no business to associate with pure girls. We are all glad to see him return to the Father's house, and we should place no obstacle before his progress toward reformation and a better life, but he must not marry my daughter. While the door of salvation stands open, and God is merciful and long suffering toward all sinners of every type, yet repentance, prayers and tears will not kill the poisonous germs. Young women, would you know the most direct route to the operating table and a premature death? Then I should say to you, marry that young man who has been sowing his wild oats. A Chicago physician recently made the statement that a young woman whose lover had a sore on his lip which he called a "cold sore," was permitted to kiss her and the results were that in three years she had rotted into her grave as the result of the intimacies of that night.

A reformed profligate makes a poor husband, being corrupt in mind and body, and a slave to voluptuous recollections which recall the debased images of the harlots with whom he formerly associated. Many women seem to be willing to take a gambler's chance and marry such men, but more often than otherwise, they, as well as their offspring, must suffer the terrible consequences. A young man brought up in ignorance of a woman's passions, temptations and her real mission in life, and who believes that he alone has a strong sexual nature which must be gratified at any cost, is no fit subject to become the head of an ideal Christian home. Not one young man in a thousand who has "sowed his wild oats" and lived a life of dissipation for a number of years makes a desirable husband. The idea that a converted rake makes the best kind of a husband is all bosh. You might just as well say that a converted prostitute would make the best wife and mother for a chaste man and his children.

I am fully aware that many young girls get the idea that if they do not entertain young men whose morals are more or less questionable and permit undue familiarities, the young men will not go with them. In the first place, allow me to say that is simply another lie of the devil. In the second place, for you to make such a statement is to question the character of that large number of wholesome, red-blooded true-hearted, pure-minded young men in our land who have kept themselves above reproach in spite of all the blandishments of a lot of silly, empty-headed society girls who have sought to seduce them by exposing their sexual charms in the most enticing ways ever conceived by Satan since he deceived Mother Eve in the garden of Eden.

I have been saying some plain things about the profligate young men, but I want to come now to the defense of my own sex by saying that in a sense the girls and women themselves are very largely responsible for the profligacy among young men today. In fact, I am finding it much easier in many places to reach the young men with the Gospel, and now-a-days it is the young men rather than the young women that are the first to respond to the invitation to accept Christ as Savior and Lord of their lives.

I find that young men are not always responsible for "spooning" or "petting," but very often young women take the initiative in this soul-destroying business. Young girls who dance and wear low-necked dresses can be counted upon as being the aggressive offenders in these dangerous forms of spooning. The partially concealed charms of a woman have always proved to be one of the most severe temptations to sex-immorality that any man has ever been compelled to face. There will be literally millions of men in hell because of a large group of half-dressed, jazz-drunk, cocktail-drinking, dance-crazy, frivolous, short-haired, flapper girls that infest the saloons and places of amusement in these days of fast living and low moral standards. I find that the average young man is more careful about his associations than is the average girl.

I think that sometimes even engaged professing Christian girls do not realize the dangers of permitting undue familiarities, forgetting that their bodies are the temples of the Holy Spirit, and must be kept clean and pure—not only for her husband to be, but for her Lord and Saviour Jesus Christ. The effects of spooning are not only dangerous to morals, but the physical and sexual results are disastrous. When indulged in even to a very limited extent, it is fraught with the severest temptations to immorality. Then in a man, if persisted in, spooning leads to unsatisfied sexual excitement resulting in aches and pains which are the forerunners of varicose veins and seminal weakness that may result in temporary or permanent sterility. It is no less injurious to women for it leads often to ovarian troubles and a wasting of nervous energy. All these things are further illustrations of the power of the mind over the physical.

"Oh," says some one, "if we girls set us such high standards as you are advocating, I am afraid many of us will live and die 'old maids'!" Well, I should answer that argument in the first place by saying: Don't worry if you don't marry, for there are things a million times worse than being an old maid, so-called, and one of those is marrying the wrong man. Some of the noblest women in all history have been our consecrated Christian maiden ladies. However, I don't call them "old maids." They are simply "ladies in waiting." Better a thousand times that you should be a maiden-lady than be yoked up with a profane, cigarette smoking, whiskey-soaked jug handle for a husband. There are many such men running loose that ought to be arrested for going around disguised as men.

In the second place, I should say that if you have given your heart to Christ and consecrated your life to Him, He is far more interested in your future than you yourself could possibly be. Put your standards high, yield yourself wholly to the will of God and make your future a matter of earnest prayer. You may be sure that God is far more interested in having His divine purpose carried out in your life than you yourself could possibly be. For years before I met my life-companion, I had been praying that the Lord would show me the one He had chosen to share the joys and sorrows of wedded life with His humble servant. To make a long story short, I would say that I have never had the least doubt but what my prayer was abundantly answered.

A fellow evangelist, Rev. John E. Brown, tells of an incident that came under his observation, which shows what resulted in the experience of a Christian girl who was known for her beauty, for her modesty and refinement. She frankly admitted that the story he had heard was true, how that on one occasion a certain young man who had been visiting her home for several months, had sought to kiss her, and she had slapped his jaws and ordered him to go home and kiss his mother. She modestly remarked, "Some day I expect to meet the man whom I am privileged to call husband, and when that time comes I want to know, and I want him to know, that I have saved all I have of purity, modesty, and affection for him."

At the State capitol, over a hundred miles away, there lived a wealthy young man, who, too, was as straight as an arrow and clean as a hound's tooth. Through certain channels this story came to his ears, and to the utter amazement of his friends, he immediately announced that he was leaving for that city, at least to have the privilege of seeing that girl, whether he ever got to know her or not.

To make a long story short, it was not "love at first sight," but love upon an acquaintanceship that resulted in deep devotion to each other and the establishment of a most wonderful home, with a happy and contented father, a beautiful, healthy wife, and several wonderful children which God sent to complete the joy and the rejoicing of the parents' hearts.

There is a proverb which reads, "All marriages are made in heaven." But, needless to say, this is not

a Biblical proverb, for certainly there are many marriages with which God never had anything to do. I
fear too many of them are like one I heard of where
the husband said, "Well, she couldn't get any husband,
and I couldn't get any wife, so the two of us just got
married." Girls, don't let your actions advertise "Man
wanted quick," for that is the surest way of not getting
a real one. You might get something with pantaloons
on, but that is not necessarily a man, let alone being
a real gentleman.

A young lady who returned from a Summer resort,
to which her mother sent her, hoping that her daughter
might gain—not health, but a husband. At the end of
the season she came home, bringing with her a little
bullet-headed, spindle-shanked card-playing, dance-hall-
mad dude, whose judgment never seemed to rise higher
than to determine which necktie he should wear in season. Fully realizing that she had not made much of
a catch, she half apologized to some of her girl friends,
"I know he isn't anything very great, but some of the
girls at the beach didn't get any." Poor little society
miss, she thought she must hurry, therefore she jumped
at the first chance. However, this couple was pretty
well matched, for a godless, worldly-minded, card-
playing, dancing, irreligious girl would be hopeless as
a wife and mother.

In spite of the fact that next to our conversion
and eternal salvation the most important step is that
of marriage, many have made a joke and farce out
of this divinely appointed institution of wedlock. Therefore it is not surprising to find sorrow, heartbreak and
matrimonial disaster on every hand. In speaking of a
Christian woman Paul said, "She is at liberty to be

married to whom she will; only in the Lord" (I Corinthians 7: 39).

The Bible forbids Christian women marrying unsaved men, or Christian men marrying unsaved women. Neither do I believe in Protestants marrying Roman Catholics or Roman Catholics marrying Protestants. There is no doubt that God intended every soul should have its mate, which, when found, will make the two truly "one flesh," but if there is to be an ideal home there must be spiritual agreement and harmony as well as being perfectly adapted to each other in oneness of thought, of desire and purpose of life. God distinctly says, "Be ye not unequally yoked together with unbelievers: for what fellowship hath righteousness with unrighteousness? and what communion hath light with darkness?" (II Corinthians 6: 14).

In one of our Montana campaigns a woman came forward one night to renew her faith, and the next morning she called me up to tell me how she still had bitterness in her heart toward God. I said, "What is your trouble?" She said, "My husband has gone away and left me with a child two years of age to provide for, and it seems unjust that God should have permitted this great sorrow and disaster to come into my life." I said, "Were you a Christian when you married this man?" She said, "I was." "Was he a professing Christian before you married him?" I inquired. "No," said she, "he was an unbeliever." "Well, then," I said, "what did you expect?" and quoted the above Scripture to her. "But," said she, "I didn't know that passage was in the Bible." "Being a Christian," I said, "you should have known. Ignorance caused by neglect excuses no one—not even in the laws of man—and here you have been trying to blame God and make Him responsible for something you have brought upon yourself through wilful disobedience to a law and a principle of righteousness which He has established for the good of His people everywhere."

I have found many women who have lost their faith in this same manner. They have tried to place the responsibility for some misfortune or time of sorrow and suffering which has come into their lives, upon a holy and righteous God, when they themselves were wholly to blame because of having ignorantly disobeyed the plain teachings of His Word. Under no circumstance should a child of God think of marrying an unsaved person. Since it is the woman rather than the man— who is the guilty party in this particular respect—I believe that fifty to seventy-five per cent of the wrecked homes in this country would have been prevented if women had understood and lived up to this principle of righteousness established by Almighty God. There is one thing sure and certain, that if you marry a child of the devil you are sure to have trouble with your father-in-law.

In these days of compromise and loose living I find many of our professing Christian girls are imbued with the idea that they can reform or convert the young men after marriage. No, you can't. It doesn't work that way in one case out of five hundred. If a man does not quit drinking, smoking and give up his sinful ways and become a Christian before he is married, you can bank on it, that he won't do it afterward. If a young man has not proved himself to be an out and out Christian for Christ's sake, you may be sure that he will never do it because of his professed loyalty and love for you. The exceptional case that you may be able to point out here and there only proves the rule.

How could a Christian girl reasonably expect God to bless her testimony while she is deliberately disobedient to the plain teachings of His Word respecting the separated life. Certainly God is both able and willing to make His will known to His children, and especially in that which is of such tremendous importance to us for both time and eternity. Let every Christian girl stand her ground and look to God for a perfect fulfillment of His will in her life. "Trust in Jehovah with all thy heart; and lean not upon thine own understanding; In all thy ways acknowledge Him, and He shall direct (make plain) thy paths" (Prov. 3: 5, 6).

Every worthwhile young man, whether he admits it or not, has the greatest respect for the young woman who lives and dares to stand up and defend her Christian principles. In one of our Minnesota campaigns a beautiful, highly respected young woman who was engaged to a prosperous young business man, was genuinely saved. Although, so far as known, the young man was morally clean and above reproach, he was not a Christian. He did not attend church, neither would he come with the young woman to any of the revival services.

This young lady was present the afternoon I spoke to "women only," and seemed deeply impressed with the teachings of God's Word respecting the separated life and the consequences of being "unequally yoked together with unbelievers." When she discovered the young man's antipathy to Christ and the church and was unsuccessful in her attempts to lead him into the Christian life, the engagement was broken. This was very much to the chagrin and regret of the young man for he loved the girl, and down in his heart he respected her all the more because of the firm stand she had taken.

A little more than a year and a half later I was in a campaign in a nearby city, and was delighted to recognize in the audience, from time to time, a number of friends and converts of the former campaign. I also rejoiced to see that the young busines man who had been turned down by his former fiancee was among the visitors and he seemed to be very deeply interested. To the delight of his friends, one evening he walked down to the front to confess Christ publicly as his Lord and Saviour, and was genuinely saved as his after life showed.

Feeling that everything would be all right, now that he had become a Christian, he went almost immediately to the young woman and asked for a renewal of the engagement. But she must have been from Missouri— the "show me" State. She said, "No, you will have to prove to me that you were moved to make your profession of faith out of love to Christ my Saviour, and not because of any wrong motives." And another whole year went by before she became thoroughly convinced by his activities in the service of Christ and the church that he meant business.

To make a long story short, they were married in a little more than a year after the young man's conversion. I met this young man some years later. His countenance simply radiated the joy and happiness that filled his heart as he told me of the wonderful way in which the Lord had blessed them in their beautiful Christian home. Some fifteen years later I was back in that town for a Bible Conference, and although this couple had moved to another city with its larger business opportunities, I found that they had left behind them a good report of a wonderful moral and spiritual influence they had had upon that community. In fact a nice new and greatly enlarged church practically owed its existence to the faithful services of this young couple. It cost that young lady many a heartache, and no doubt there were times when she questioned the wisdom of the courageous stand she had taken. But the Lord richly blessed and greatly honored and rewarded her faith and trust, just as He will that of any young woman who is willing to trust her future with Him, "For the Lord God is a sun and a shield; the Lord will give grace and glory: no good thing will He withhold from them that walk uprightly" (Psalm 84: 11).

CHAPTER IX.

A VIRTUOUS WOMAN AND THE CHRISTIAN HOME

"Then said he, What have they seen in thine house? And Hezekiah answered, All that is in mine house have they seen: there is nothing among my treasures that I have not shewed them."—ISAIAH 39: 4.

KING Hezekiah had been sick, nigh unto death, but had been miraculously restored by a special providence of God. When the King of Babylon heard of this remarkable restoration of the king's health, he sent his son and other messengers with a present and letters of congratulation to King Hezekiah at Jerusalem. It was a splendid opportunity for King Hezekiah to witness to the goodness and mercy of God, but instead of giving honor and glory to God he seemed to be thinking only of his material prosperity. "And showed them the house of his precious things, the silver, and the gold, and the spices, and the precious ointment, and all the house of his armour, and all that was found in his treasures."

Of course, what these messengers saw in Hezekiah's house would determinate their estimate of the king in the eyes of those worldly men. Just so, if you will tell me what you have in your home, I will be able to tell the world what kind of parents you are, what kind of children you have, the kind of home you have and what kind of influence you are exerting in the world for good or evil. Therefore, taking this question, "What have they seen in thine house?" as a starting point, I wish to have you think with me for a little while of that place which knows more sweet associations and pleasant memories than any other spot on earth—the Christian home.

The home was the first divine institution that Jehovah planted upon this earth. It came into existence before the school, the church or the state, and if we could settle the home question right we would be able to settle all other questions in a way and manner that would give us a heaven-on-earth immediately. Our national life will never rise higher than our best homes, and will never fall lower than our worst homes. Your city or community is on a level with your homes, and your homes are on a level with your women. A town never falls below its worst women and never rises higher than its best women. Men may build their houses and provide for the material things of life, but the women make or unmake the home. Therefore, "What have they seen in thine house?"

In Ephesians 5: 22-33, Paul gives us a God-inspired revelation of that which constitutes an ideal Christian home, that is, in so far as the relationships of the husband and the wife are concerned. "Wives, submit yourselves unto your husbands, as unto the Lord. For the husband is the head of the wife, even as Christ is the head of the church: and he is the saviour of the body. Therefore as the church is subject unto Christ, so let the wives be to their own husbands in every thing. Husbands, love your wives, even as Christ also loved the church, and gave himself for it . . . So ought men to love their wives as their own bodies. . . . For this cause shall a man leave his father and mother, and shall be joined unto his wife, and they two shall be one flesh . . . Nevertheless let every one of you in particular so love his wife even as himself; and the wife see that she reverence her husband."

According to this Scripture—which I have quoted at length because of its tremendous importance—a home to be ideal must have at its head a Christian husband and father. The entrance of sin into this world through the fall of Adam and Eve—which brought disorder and interruption of God's original plan for the human family—made necessary a headship, and that headship is vested in man. Neither man nor woman has ever been able to successfully change God's order at this point, although many have tried to accomplish that very thing in this wicked generation. Particularly has this been true on the part of a certain class of women who have tried to throw off all restraint and gain a so-called freedom and liberty that she imagined would be ideal. However, in her attempt to escape that sphere of life and responsibility to which she was divinely ordained by God Himself, women have certainly made one grand, glorious mess of things politically, religiously, morally, and spiritually and we see a state of chaos in society today almost equal to that which prevailed upon this earth before the Noahic flood: "And God saw that the wickedness of man was great in the earth, and that every imagination of the thoughts of his heart was only evil continually" (Gen. 6: 5).

The men of this generation are very much the same as they have been for many generations past, but since the World War there has been a very decided change in the attitude and conduct of women both morally and spiritually. This is indeed a sad state of affairs, and especially since it is a fact that women have it within their power either to make or destroy the nation according to their attitude toward their divinely appointed sphere in life. History reveals the fact that no great nation has ever been destroyed until its women were first enticed to turn from their God-given mission—that is, the making of the home. And unless something can be done to save the women of our country from their terrible carnival of drunkenness and licentiousness our nation is just as certain to sink into oblivion as the sun is to rise in the heavens tomorrow morning. No individual or nation need hope to succeed so long as they continue to transgress the laws and principles of righteousness established by Almighty God for the perpetuation of the family and the Christian home.

Do not think for one moment that I am trying to excuse the men for their part in this world tragedy, neither am I trying to say that the women are inferior to the men, mentally or intellectually, but I am trying to show that to a very large extent women must be held responsible for the breaking up and breaking down of world conditions politically, morally and spiritually. This is due to her search for the so-called freedom she feels she has been denied hitherto. Women have actually—consciously or unconsciously—endeavored to defeat the divine purpose for which God created man and woman in the beginning. Men and women were created different because it was God's purpose that they should carry out two entirely different missions in life. This is manifested even in their physique— the man has greater physical strength while the woman is of a finer physical texture because she must of necessity take the more prominent part in procreation and the perpetuity of the human race.

The proper relationships of husbands and wives are clearly set forth in First Peter 3: 1-7, R.V. This passage, as well as the one quoted above, in no sense implies that women are inferior to the men either physically or intellectually. In both cases the inspired writers are dealing with the obligations of both the man and the woman according to the different spheres of life to which they were ordained of God in the beginning. I have space here for only a small part of this latter passage and because of the unwarranted criticism on the part of some over enthusiastic contenders for so-called women's rights, I suggest that you turn to your Bible and read for yourselves: "In like manner, ye wives, be in subjection to your own husbands; that, even if any obey not the word, they may without the word be gained by the behaviour of their wives; beholding your chaste behaviour coupled with fear. . . . Ye husbands, in like manner, dwell with your wives according to knowledge, giving honor unto the woman, as unto the weaker vessel, as being joint-heirs of the grace of life; to the end that your prayers be not hindered."

In recent years we find many wives in rebellion against the teachings of both Paul and Peter respecting their obligation to "be in subjection" unto their husbands. However, in both passages quoted above we see that marriage is a matter of give and take—not all take nor all give on the part of either husband or wife. Certainly neither passage should be construed to mean that the wife is to be a slave to her husband, or that the husband is to lord it over the wife like a slave-driver. However, in these days we do not find so very many husbands who are trying to be a so-called "boss," anyway. It is too often the other way.

You have probably heard that story of the farmer who was determined to find out who was the boss in the homes of his community. He hitched his two horses to his wagon and took along a number of chickens. He went through the settlement making inquiry at each home as to which was boss, the husband or wife. If they both admitted that the wife was boss, he gave them a chicken, but if he found a home in which the husband was jointly admitted to be the boss he intended to present them with a horse. After presenting a number of couples with a chicken, he finally came to a home where both admitted that the husband was the boss of that home. "All right," said the farmer, "which horse do you want, the black or the gray?" The husband said, "I will take the black horse." Just then the wife called her husband into the next room for a little conference. When they returned the husband said, "We have decided to take the gray horse." "No, you won't," said the old farmer, "you also get a chicken."

From my observation and experience in dealing with many husbands and wives who were on the point of separation, I fear most of them would have to be content with a chicken. As someone has expressed it: "A home to be ideal should be like an orchestra with every instrument in tune and every player doing his part, and doing it well. But alas! far too often we find the home is more like a mutiny. The husband in mutiny against the wife, the wife in mutiny against her husband. The children in mutiny against the parents, and the parents in mutiny against the children. Quarreling, discord, and strife, casting a gloom over the whole house."

However, we do sometimes find a home with harmony, but without affection and love—the harmony of a cold, lifeless machine. It would seem that most young men know intuitively how to make love in the days of youth and courtship, but forget all about it very soon after the wedding ceremony is over. Too many, both husbands and wives, are keeping their alabaster boxes of love and tenderness sealed up until that grim messenger "death" has visited the home. But I would say to you women that one little buttonhole bouquet that the wife pins upon the husband's coat with loving hands, will do far more to make love in that home of yours than a cart-load of "florists' sheaves" or "broken harps" or "open books" or "rest in peace" piled on his coffin. Many homes would be much happier if they had a little more "taffy" and not so much "epitaffy."

> *" 'Tis by far a better way,*
> *To buy a cheap bouquet today,*
> *Than a bushel of roses white and red,*
> *To lay on his coffin when he is dead."*

No doubt many husbands would say "Amen" to the sentiment expressed in that verse, but you must not forget that probably if your wife should express what is in her heart, today, she would probably say:

"Give me a rosebud,
A rosebud pink or red.
I would rather have just one today
Than ten thousand when I am dead."

Again I ask the prophets' question, "What have
they seen in thy house?" The purpose of marriage
and the home is the propagation of the human race.
Therefore I would ask, "Have they seen in thy house
the smiling faces of those children which you have
welcomed as a precious gift from God?" No home
can be complete without a baby. "Lo, children are
an heritage of the Lord: and the fruit of the womb
is his reward. . . . Happy is the man that hath his
quiver full of them: they shall not be ashamed, but
they shall speak with the enemies in the gate" (Psalm
127:3, 5).

The Hebrew women considered children to be God's
greatest possible gift to them, and the greatest disappointment that could come to any Hebrew wife was
to be childless. As I have already tried to make plain
in a previous chapter, the greatest privilege of any
real man is to be a father, and the greatest honor that
can come to a wedded woman is to be a mother. But
alas! many children are received into this world in
these days as burdensome charges and are handicapped
throughout life by having had the word "Unwelcome"
indelibly and clearly written upon their sad faces. But
we can all thank God for the many exceptions we find
here and there. Laying aside his own plans for life
while yet a mere lad, the late Rev. John McNeil, one
of Scotland's greatest preachers, went home from school
one day, and said, "Mother, I am going to be a

preacher." Her pale face lighted up with joy as she drew him down and kissed him as she said, "Johnny dear, I meant you for that long before I saw your face." She had never told him before. Yes, praise God, we still have a few Hannahs left in the world.

In a wealthy little city in the middle west a prominent young business man came to evangelist John E. Brown with this question, "Can able-bodied, well-to-do young couples be Christians when they deliberately and cold-bloodedly refuse to assume the responsibility of parenthood, and are shutting the baby from the home?" My friend answered as I have answered a number who have asked me the same question, "They can not!" This young man said, "That is my conviction, but my wife is a professing Christian, and sings in the choir, and she is urging me to take a stand and join the church. I have always wanted children but she refuses to assume the responsibilities of motherhood. In our set there are about twenty-five couples who have been married from five to twelve years, and amongst those twenty-five couples there is only one child; and practically every one of these couples is doing just what we are doing."

To keep our native-born population at its present figure, requires an average of four children per each married couple. Our land is being populated by poverty and ignorance and we see evidences everywhere of the deterioration of our nation, politically, morally and spiritually. How few children come into the world today as a result of earnest desire, design and prayer. I am fully aware that not every childless home is childless by choice, but woe be unto them that are! To avoid criticism and the possibility of becoming a stumbling block to an unsaved world, I feel that those who are childless through no fault of their own, should make it known through adopting one or more children. If this be impossible for reasons best known to themselves, then in some manner their disappointment should be made known lest their Christian testimony be hindered.

Having been conceived in love and born of a pious, praying mother, the next greatest blessing that can possibly come to any child is that of being reared in an ideal Christian home. The greatest factor in my conversion and entrance into the Christian ministry was that of being born and reared by an old-fashioned godly mother of nine children, eight of whom grew up into manhood and womanhood. The influence of her godly example and teachings have followed me to this day and any blessing that may have come to millions to whom I have had the privilege of preaching the Gospel, and the scores of thousands that have publicly confessed Christ under my ministry can be traced to the fact that I was conceived, born, and reared by a godly, praying mother.

Therefore, any mother who wishes to send her children out into the world with a proper estimate of the value and safety there is for young people in the Christian life, must live the Christ-life herself. To me one of the greatest monstrosities on this earth is to see a mother with a number of children growing up around her, who is not herself a consecrated Christian. The greatest of all preachers since Paul, Charles Haddon Spurgeon of London, once said to his students: "When I am gone all sorts of people will write my life. They will have some difficulty in accounting for the position

God has given me. I can tell you two reasons why I am what I am." He paused and then slowly and thoughtfully added, "My mother and the truth of my message." And so has it been with great men and women of affairs back through the history of Christendom—they were mother-made.

"If I had all the mothers I ever saw to choose from, I would have chosen you," said Thomas Carlyle, in a letter to his mother. "All that I am, all that I hope to be, I owe to my angel mother—blessings on her memory! I remember my mother's prayers. They have always followed me. They have clung to me all my life," said Abraham Lincoln. "If my mother could rise in the dead of night and pray for my recovery from sickness, my life must be worth something. I then and there resolved to prove myself worthy of my mother's prayers," said James A. Garfield, one of our martyred presidents. "I should have become an atheist but for one recollection, and that was the memory of the time when my departed mother used to take my little hand in hers and cause me on my knees to say, 'Our Father, who art in heaven'," so said John Randolph.

The late Honorable John Wanamaker, a prince among the greatest merchants of the last century, Philadelphia's most honorable Christian layman, wrote the following tribute to his mother after he was eighty years of age: "My first love was my mother, and my first home was on her breast. My first bed was upon her bosom. Leaning little arms upon her knees, I learned my first prayers. A bright lamp she lighted in my soul, that never dies down nor goes out, though the winds and waves of fourscore years have swept over me. Sitting in my mother's old armchair which she loved—

because her firstborn son gave it to her forty years ago—I am writing this in the evening twilight. With the darkness falling, I seem to lose myself in the flood of sweet memories, and to feel that the arms of the chair have loosed themselves to become my very own mother's arms around me again, drawing me to her bosom, the happiest place on earth, just as she used to do in the days and nights long gone by. I feel the touch of her little hand on my brow, and I hear her voice as she smooths my hair and calls me her boy, her very own boy."

Of course no such tributes to mother can be hoped for where the mother is a card fiend and the father belongs to half a dozen clubs and lodges and the parents are so busy with their social affairs they hardly have time to get acquainted with their own children. Unless your children find a real church in their home, they are not likely ever to find a home in the church. Many years ago a prominent citizen sent out a challenge, defying any mother who is a devotee of the card game to produce either a great son or daughter. This challenge has never been met for it is claimed that no woman card fiend in the history of America has ever given the nation a great son or daughter. The reason for this is that there is no factor so potent in the salvation or damnation of a child's life as the influence and example of a mother in the home.

There is little use praying for that fellow running the booze joint until we can get professing Christian mothers unjointed from the card table and that daughter of hers disjointed from the ball room. We are told that in a town in Illinois a mother living on one of its finest avenues came in the front door of her home one afternoon with a ten-dollar pitcher that she had won at a parlor card game, and at the same hour her son came in at the back door with a ten-dollar bill he had won at a saloon and gambling joint. They both played the same game and with the same kind of cards, and in the sight of God and the laws of our land, both were gamblers.

After a traveling salesman, who was a member of the Gideons, had given an address in one of the fashionable churches of Chicago, he was approached by a sad-faced mother who asked him if he would be in Auburn, New York, soon. He said, "Yes, I expect to be there in a few weeks." The woman handed him a photograph of herself and a letter for her son who was in the penitentiary at Auburn. She said, "He never answers my letters and I hope you will be so kind as to deliver these to my son with my love."

When the traveling man reached Auburn he went to the penitentiary and asked for the young man. He was brought into the office and after looking intently at the photograph he said, "Yes, that's my mother. Her hair is grayer than when I saw her last. Doubtless my conduct has put many of those gray hairs there. Are you going back to Chicago soon?" asked the young man. "Yes, in about ninety days," said the traveling salesman. Handing the photograph back to the salesman, and also the letter, which he refused to read, he said, "Take these back to my mother. I do not want them here. It was in my mother's home that I played my first game of cards. It was at my mother's table I took my first drink of liquor. Drinking and gambling have put me here for fifteen years. After having pushed me behind prison bars by her godless example she dares to send me her photograph and pretended love. Take these back and tell my mother that I damn her and the religion she professes." And turning to the guard in charge, he said, "Take me back to my cell." Can you imagine that poor mother's feeling upon receiving a charge like that from her son for whose downfall she was personally responsible? But that is not the end. Think of the eternal consequence of a wrong example in the home.

In a fashionable home a young daughter was dying. The mother's heart was breaking and she cried out in despair: "O God, save my child!" The dying daughter turned to her and uttered these terrible words: "Mother dear, it is too late now! You made me learn to dance, to go to theaters and operas, and move in society. Your only ambition for me was that I might shine as a society belle. But you never read the Bible to me; you never took me to prayer meeting; you never had me take part in the activities of the church. Our church going once a Sabbath was a formal matter, and we went because our set did. You never talked to me of the Saviour, and now I'm dying—O God, dying!" And she took that awful leap into eternity a lost soul all because of her mother's desire to have her daughter shine as a society belle here on earth rather than to be among the redeemed in that day when our Lord shall come to make up His jewels. "Favor is deceitful, and beauty is vain: but a woman that feareth the Lord, she shall be praised" (Proverbs 31: 30).

However, I do not want to close my message to the mothers of our nation with these dark pictures. Several years ago, five young men left their homes in a Western Pennsylvania town and went out into the great Northwest. They found things quite different from what they were in the old home town, and the temptations were many. Some time later they had all returned to their former homes. Four of the five showed that they were much the worse because of their experiences in a strange country. But the other young man came back seemingly all the stronger and better because of the experiences through which he had passed.

When asked why he, too, had not gone the way of the other four, he calmly replied, "Because I carried with me a picture." "Oh, yes, the picture of some young maiden back home, I presume?" remarked a friend. "Oh, no! Not that kind of a picture," said the young man. "It was a picture of quite a different kind. It was my last morning at home. We all sat down to breakfast as usual; father at one end of the table and my precious mother at the other. Realizing that there was to be a breaking of home ties in a few hours, conversation was not very brisk that morning. After breakfast, as was my father's custom, he took down the old Bible and started to read the morning lesson. But he didn't get very far. A lump kept coming up in his throat, and he was so blinded by tears that he could not read, and handed the book over to my mother, motioning to her to finish the reading.

"After she had finished the chapter we all knelt to pray. Father started his prayer as was his custom, but he didn't get far until that same lump came up in his throat and choked back further expression. Then mother reached over and put her hand on my shoulder and began to pray, saying, 'O God we thank thee for our son. We thank thee for our son. We thank thee that thou has kept him true and faithful, and that we are able to send him out from our home chaste and clean. Keep him pure and clean and may his feet never stray from the paths of virtue, purity and the truth in which we have tried to bring him up. Bring him back to us as pure and true as he is going out from us.' It was the vision of my last morning in the atmosphere of a godly home and the remembrance of my precious mother's prayer. I could not bear the thought of breaking the heart of my father and mother and dishonoring my Lord and Saviour Jesus Christ whom they taught me to love."

Many Christian parents are deeply concerned about their children—and well might they be in these days when there are so many evil influences at work to destroy the homes of our land. The evils which the rising generation must face were never so numerous as at the present time. Atheism, Communism and Antichristianity are in evidence everywhere. The enemies of Christ and the home are not growing less, they are becoming more and more numerous today than ever before and are constantly increasing. Therefore, parents should understand that no boy or girl is safe in these times who is not a Christian. It should also be made clear to the young people, that to be a Christian means separation from the world, the flesh and the devil. Yes, it means just that and nothing less, for it is either a whole Christ or no Christ, we either crown Him Lord of all in our lives or we do not crown Him at all. "For bodily exercise profiteth little: but godliness is profitable unto all things, having promise of the life that now is, and of that which is to come" (I Timothy 4:8).

Printed in the United States of America